WHISKING WAFER & SILICON SOUFFLÉS

WHISKING WAFER & SILICON SOUFFLÉS

HOW CULINARY CHAOS CAN REVOLUTIONIZE YOUR SUPPLY CHAIN STRATEGY

JULIEN CHEN

Julien Chen
Whisking Wafer & Silicon Soufflés
How Culinary Chaos Can Revolutionize Your Supply Chain Strategy

Published by Spines
ISBN: 979-8-89950-855-4

Spines

CONTENTS

ABOUT THE AUTHOR

J CHEN

From running a restaurant to navigating the complexities of global trade, I've lived at the intersection of chaos and strategy. As a former restaurant owner, international global merchant, and retailer, I've managed everything from high-volume, low-mix consumer products to the intricate demands of high-mix, low-volume semiconductor supply chains. I've led massive operations across countries, overseeing manufacturing of diverse materials, cross-border logistics planning, cost optimization, quality control, on-time delivery, financial performance, and staffing. I've also established operational sites in culturally distinct environments around the world. My approach blends critical thinking with bold, strategic formulation — and my passion lies in building systems that don't just withstand pressure, but evolve because of it.

I'm J. Chen, and this is my first book—built on real burn marks earned in both the kitchen and the boardroom.

From plating dishes during the dinner rush in a packed restaurant to orchestrating multi-million-dollar shipments across continents, I've learned a simple truth: resilience doesn't come from avoiding chaos; it comes from designing with it in mind.

This book is the culmination of a journey across flavors and forecasts, sauté pans and semiconductor fabs—an exploration of how creativity, precision, and adaptability can transform any operation into something unforgettable.

> "If the fire's already there, you might as well cook something worth serving."

AUTHOR'S NOTE: FROM THE KITCHEN TO THE CLEANROOM

When I first walked into a commercial kitchen years ago, I learned fast that success wasn't just about ingredients—it was about rhythm, resilience, and respect for the process. Decades later, walking through semiconductor fabs in cleanroom boots and bunny suits, I felt that same heartbeat. Precision. Pressure. Pride in craft. And above all, teamwork.

This book began as a metaphor—a fun way to connect my culinary past with my supply chain present. But as I stirred deeper, I realized the metaphor wasn't just convenient; it was powerful. Both worlds require planning under pressure. Both demand constant iteration. Both are fueled by people who care deeply about the result, even if their names aren't on the final plate.

"Whisking Wafers & Silicon Soufflés" is more than just a guide to procurement strategies, lean principles, or green innovation. It's a celebration of the creativity, courage, and collaboration that define supply chain excellence. It's a love letter to the operators who rework a process at midnight, the planners who stay ahead of the burn, and the sourcing teams who turn scarcity into opportunity.

To the chefs of the supply chain—thank you for your hunger to improve, your willingness to fail forward, and your ability to make even the most chaotic kitchen hum. I hope this book made you laugh, think, and maybe even see your role with new flavor.

And as for what's next? Keep your knives sharp. Keep your curiosity sharper. The next recipe is already simmering.

Bon appétit—now and always.

— J. Chen, Global Supply Chain Management,
Cleanroom Chef & Culinary Strategist at Heart

DEDICATION

*To my mother, **Alice Guo** —*

The first chef in my life's kitchen.

You taught me that love is measured not in teaspoons,

but in the quiet patience of slow simmering,

the resilience to stir through the burn,

and the courage to serve what comes from the heart.

From you, I learned that even the most intricate circuits

need a steady current to come alive —

just as every recipe needs your warmth to rise.

Every whisk, every plate, every page here carries your flavor.

This book is seasoned with your strength,

and I dedicate it wholly to you.

ACKNOWLEDGMENTS

Every great dish is rarely the work of a single chef—and this book was no different. *It was a banquet made possible by mentors, colleagues, friends, and family who inspired, challenged, and cheered every step of the journey.*

To every team member who stayed late to debug a material issue, to every supplier who took a chance on an untested idea, and to every leader who believed that supply chain strategy could also be soulful—thank you.

Special thanks to the mentors and colleagues who inspired the culinary metaphors and supported this book's journey from brainstorming to bookplate: Debra Matsuhiro, Mahmut Gunar, Whiter Hsieh, Agnes Shih, Jackson Chao, and Kevin Chiu. Your guidance was the perfect mise en place.

To Amy Yan—the steady flame behind every bold leap, impossible deadline, and late-night brainstorm. You never questioned the chaos; you embraced it and stood beside it. This book holds your belief between the lines.

To my sourcing family, executives, engineering partners, and operations teams around the world—this is your book as much as it is mine. Your grit, brilliance, and commitment to excellence have seasoned every chapter.

And finally, to every reader who picked up this book with curiosity and an appetite for transformation: may your own supply chain journey be as flavorful, resilient, and satisfying as a perfectly balanced dish.

Bon appétit—and thank you.

1

THE RECEIPT OF SUCCESS – INGREDIENTS OF SUPPLY CHAIN MANAGEMENT

Welcome to the Kitchen: Where Strategy Meets Sizzle

BEFORE THE SOUFFLÉS rise and the wafers crisp, before the silicon simmers and the logic flows—there's prep. And not just any prep. Think mise en place on an industrial scale. In the culinary world, the best meals aren't born from chaos; they're composed like symphonies—each note (or nut, bolt, and wafer) precisely placed. Likewise, a successful supply chain doesn't just happen. It's designed, tested, refined, and, yes—occasionally "flambéed."

Your supply chain is your kitchen. And like any great kitchen, it runs on ingredients, tools, timing, and people. If the sauté station is backed up, the entire dish gets delayed. If the walk-in is missing produce, you're pivoting to plan B on the fly. In the same way, a delay in a shipment of substrates can bring a multimillion-dollar semiconductor line to a screeching halt.

In this opening chapter, we whisk through the five fundamental ingredients of any supply chain strategy—Manpower, Materials, Machines, Methods, and Measurements. Or as we like to call them: the

Five M's of Operational Mise en Place. Like flour, eggs, and butter, each of these must be balanced, managed, and blended to produce something exceptional.

Let's step into the kitchen.

Mise en Place: Manpower (People) as the First Ingredient

Every Michelin-starred kitchen has a secret ingredient. Spoiler alert: it's not truffle oil. It's the people. The brigade behind the pass line. The dishwasher who keeps the rhythm. The sous-chef who finishes your sentence with a squeeze of lemon. In supply chain management, it's no different. People power the process. And when that human ingredient is missing or misaligned, even the best strategy falls flat like an under-whipped meringue.

Think of your global team as your culinary dream crew. The demand planner in Austin is your garde-manger, prepping forecasts with precision. The supplier quality engineer in Penang is your saucier, refining raw inputs into compliant perfection. And your site leader in Dresden? They're the executive chef—keeping everything firing in rhythm and sync.

In the semiconductor space, the stakes are even higher. A shortage of skilled operators can stall output as fast as a broken mixer in mid-service. With tools costing millions and tolerances thinner than filo dough, talent isn't a luxury—it's the foundation. That's why investing in training, cross-skilling, and workforce resilience isn't just HR policy; it's survival seasoning.

Building a world-class supply chain starts with this one simple truth: the right people, in the right roles, with the right mindset, make everything else possible. You wouldn't trust a pastry intern to butcher a wagyu ribeye. Likewise, you don't assign a cost analyst to manage wafer lot scheduling. Talent allocation is as strategic as ingredient sourcing—and just as critical to the final plate.

Materials: The Pantry of Possibilities

A chef is only as good as their ingredients. You can have the finest knives, the fastest burners, and the most elegant plating—but if your tomatoes are mealy and your herbs are wilted, the dish falls apart. The same holds true in supply chain management. Your materials are your pantry. And whether you're whipping up crème brûlée or crafting 5nm wafers, what you start with determines what you can serve.

In the semiconductor kitchen, your "ingredients" aren't flour or eggs. They're silicon substrates, rare earth elements, resins, photoresists, and specialized gases. Some come from Japan, others from South Korea, Germany, or even a cleanroom-certified warehouse in Texas. Each one is essential. Each one has a story. And if just one goes missing? It's like forgetting the yeast in your sourdough—nothing rises.

Smart supply chains treat material sourcing like a tasting menu: curated, controlled, and continuously evaluated. You need multiple suppliers for your critical components—not just to keep pricing honest, but to make sure your soufflé doesn't collapse when a key vendor gets snowed in, sanctioned, or suddenly swallowed by an acquisition. That's why dual sourcing, supplier audits, and qualification pipelines are as fundamental as knowing how to source a ripe avocado in winter.

And then there's traceability. In the culinary world, farm-to-table transparency is a sign of quality. Diners want to know if their greens were grown on a regenerative farm or flown in from halfway around the world. In semiconductor land, it's even more serious. Can you trace the origin of your ceramic capacitors? Do you know what factory blended your resist polymer? Because when a defect shows up in post-silicon validation, you can't afford to guess—it's "recipe recall" time.

Material planning is more than just a logistics game. It's supply chain gastronomy. It's about knowing which ingredients to stock deep, which to source on consignment, and which ones you need to keep temperature-controlled in bonded storage until the exact moment of release. And with longer lead times—some over a year—it's like slow-roasting a brisket: patience, planning, and precision are key.

So, before you even switch on the burners, check your pantry. A supply chain's greatness doesn't start at the fab—it starts at the loading dock, with a carefully constructed bill of materials and a sourcing strategy that sees beyond just cost.

Material Mise en Place - Prepping the Pantry for Performance

Every chef knows that the real cooking happens before the fire hits the pan. It's in the prep—the precise dicing of shallots, the neatly labeled spice jars, the ramekins of clarified butter all within arm's reach. That's mise en place. And in the supply chain kitchen, your materials need the same kind of staging and thoughtfulness. Because no matter how premium your ingredients are, if they're buried in the wrong warehouse or arrive half a day late, your whole recipe unravels.

In semiconductor operations, the margins are tight, and the timelines tighter. You're juggling multi-tiered bills of materials, hundreds of custom part numbers, and suppliers across different continents—all with their own clocks, languages, and lead times. The goal? Have everything you need exactly when you need it—not a minute early, not a minute late. Welcome to the art of material mise en place.

Think of this as the staging ground before the magic happens. It's not just about ordering parts; it's about strategic stocking. Which materials get kept in consignment? Which need safety buffers? Which are dual-sourced versus single-threaded with a known risk flag? And how do you balance all this without blowing out working capital like an overstocked walk-in?

Here's where segmentation saves the day. Just as a chef groups ingredients by prep station—meat, veg, pastry—you should be classifying your materials by criticality, lead time, and consumption rate. Your copper lead frames and gold wire might need kitting precision down to the gram, while trays and reels can ride in bulk.

High-risk resins? Maybe they live in bonded storage with release protocols tighter than a soufflé's rise time.

And don't forget internal logistics. In a fab or backend site, even the most pristine material is useless if it's on the wrong shelf. That's why line-side stocking, point-of-use inventory, and material kitting are more than lean buzzwords—they're the garnish on your plating. Done right, they keep flow humming. Done poorly, you're running back to the walk-in while the risotto turns to mush.

Material mise en place is what separates the amateurs from the artisans. It's the behind-the-scenes choreography that ensures the show runs smoothly. So don't just source your ingredients—stage them. Because even the best silicon needs its onions chopped and ready before the burners go on.

Machines - Tools of the Trade: From Knives to Nanometers

In every kitchen, tools matter. A master chef may possess perfect instincts and flawless technique, but hand them a dull knife or a warped sauté pan, and you'll still end up with uneven slices and scorched sauce. The same goes for the semiconductor supply chain. Your machines—whether in a French kitchen or a Class 1 cleanroom—can make or break the execution.

In this context, machines don't just refer to the photolithography giants and etching beasts humming away in fabs across Taiwan or Oregon. They include the precision pick-and-place robots, wafer saws, plasma ashers, AOI scanners, and the unglamorous but vital chillers, scrubbers, and vacuum pumps that keep the operation in balance. Every one of these machines is a key station in the line, like the pasta extruder or the proofing cabinet in a restaurant. If one breaks, the whole service suffers.

But here's the twist: in the kitchen, a good chef adapts. Knife dull? Grab another. Oven runs hot? Adjust your timing. In semiconductor manufacturing, there's no such luxury. The machines are hyper-specialized, painstakingly calibrated, and terrifyingly expensive. If your EUV scanner goes down, you're not pivoting to "plancha." You're watching millions in lost production drip off the line like a ruined reduction.

That's why tool uptime and maintenance planning are non-negotiable. You wouldn't run a dinner service without cleaning your grill, and you definitely wouldn't risk metal shavings from a broken food processor in someone's entrée. Likewise, you don't run a wafer line without predictive maintenance protocols, spare parts strategies, and MTBF (Mean Time Between Failures) data built into your playbook. This is where your equipment engineering team becomes your pit crew—tuning, testing, and keeping the line lean and mean.

In addition, tool utilization is a silent performance metric. Idle tools are like empty tables in prime-time dinner service—they burn cash. You need strong OEE (Overall Equipment Effectiveness), quick changeovers, and a process flow that minimizes downtime. In high-mix environments, like packaging and testing, machine flexibility becomes the name of the game. Your tools need to handle both high-volume risotto and low-volume foie gras—without choking.

And don't forget scalability. As demand grows, your toolset should be able to scale like a ghost kitchen in a viral TikTok food trend. That means knowing your throughput, expansion triggers, and tool lead times cold. A nine-month wait for a new etch chamber isn't something you can "expedite" like an overnighted lobster tail.

Sharpen those blades—literal or otherwise. Because machines aren't just tools; they're the heartbeat of your entire operation. Treat them with the respect of a prized mandoline, and they'll keep turning.

Methods - Recipes, Routines, and the Rhythm of Flow

You can have the finest ingredients and the sharpest tools, but without a recipe—or at least a well-practiced routine—you're just throwing things in a pot and hoping for the best: chaos, not cuisine. In the world of supply chains, methods are your recipes. They guide execution, ensure consistency, and allow your operation to scale without losing flavor—or, in our case, quality, yield, and delivery performance.

Just like a kitchen's standard operating procedures (SOPs)—how long to sear the scallops, when to flash the broccolini, how to rest the lamb —supply chains rely on structured methods to maintain rhythm. This includes everything from demand forecasting and production planning to order fulfillment and reverse logistics. These aren't just task lists; they're choreographed performances where timing, precision, and flow are everything.

Think of takt time as your "cook time." It's the heartbeat of production, ensuring that every workstation delivers at a pace that keeps the dish on schedule. You wouldn't let the pasta boil for 12 minutes if it only needs 8. Similarly, in semiconductor manufacturing, you can't afford for a packaging line to lag behind a burn-in station; it disrupts the entire banquet.

In a fabless or hybrid model, methods become even more critical. You're collaborating across time zones, cultures, and systems. Your recipes must be standardized but flexible, like a great chef who can substitute saffron for turmeric when needed—without compromising the final plate. This is where process mapping, control plans, and playbooks shine. When a site in the Philippines needs to mirror the output of one in Germany, your recipe book better be laminated, digital, and up to date.

And then there's the rhythm—flow. This is what separates high-functioning kitchens from headless-chicken chaos. Flow means everything arrives where it's needed, when it's needed, in the right quantity and condition. Flow is the perfect reduction that thickens at the right second—not a second before or after. In supply chains, that's Lean. That's Kanban. That's process orchestration that glides like a maître d' during the Saturday dinner rush.

Good methods allow for predictability; great methods leave room for creativity. Just as chefs riff on a classic dish, seasoned supply chain pros can adjust plans on the fly without losing sight of the core outcome: delivering value. Whether it's using digital twins for production scenarios or running tabletop simulations for crisis response, the method is not just a tool—it's your "secret sauce."

So, dust off those process charts, refine your SOPs, and embrace the rhythm. Because when your methods are tight, your kitchen sings—and your wafers, like your ravioli, come out just right.

Measurements - Tasting the Results, One KPI at a Time

Even the most dazzling dish isn't declared a success until it's tasted. A final spoonful, a raised eyebrow, a nod of approval—that's how a chef knows it's right. In supply chain management, tasting comes in the form of data. Performance isn't assumed—it's measured, analyzed, and refined like a sommelier evaluating a rare vintage. Welcome to the final "M" in our Five-Ms feast: Measurements.

In the culinary world, you might measure consistency by the doneness of a steak, the balance of seasoning, or the number of returned plates. In the supply chain kitchen, we measure cycle times, yield rates, inventory turns, OTIF (On-Time-In-Full), and dozens of other KPIs that tell us how smoothly—and deliciously—we're operating. Without these, you're cooking blindfolded.

Let's start with flavor profiling—aka data segmentation. Not every metric has the same weight on the palate. A missed OTIF ("On-Time-In-Full") in a low-mix commodity product might be a hiccup. But a 2% drop in die attach yield on your high-margin flagship chip? That's a dish-sinking disaster. Great supply chain chefs know which KPIs are appetizers and which are the main course. They prioritize the numbers that feed the business, not just the ones that fill a dashboard.

That said, measurement without action is just seasoning in the wind. Metrics should be your taste testers—constantly informing adjustments to process, people, or tools. Is your supplier performance dipping? Maybe it's time to stir the pot on your scorecard criteria. Is your lead time creeping up like a soufflé? Better check the process oven for bottlenecks. In semiconductor manufacturing, even the tiniest deviation—a one-micron shift—can turn your perfect batch into wafer waste.

Digital transformation has supercharged our ability to taste-test in real time. With IoT sensors feeding equipment utilization data and AI models predicting stockouts, you can go from gut feel to gourmet insight in seconds. It's the equivalent of having a sous-chef who whispers, "Don't plate yet—the scallop's not quite ready." Actionable, immediate, and accurate.

And don't forget the team. Just like front-of-house and back-of-house share service metrics to keep diners happy, your supply chain crew should share aligned KPIs across functions. When procurement, planning, logistics, and production all cook to the same metrics, you eliminate finger-pointing and elevate collaboration. Everyone becomes a stakeholder in the same recipe.

So, taste often, measure wisely, and adjust boldly. Because at the end of the day, your supply chain's success isn't about how pretty the plating looks on paper—it's about how it performs under the pressure of the pass. Data doesn't lie; it just tells you when to turn up the heat.

Finishing the Plate: From Ingredients to Interaction

Now that we've stocked the pantry, sharpened the knives, aligned the team, and plated our performance, it's time to step back and admire the mise en place. You've seen how each of the Five M's—Manpower, Materials, Machines, Methods, and Measurements—contribute to the symphony of supply chain excellence. But here's the twist: ingredients alone don't make a meal. It's what you do with them—and who you do it with—that elevates the outcome from functional to unforgettable.

In the kitchen, even the most exquisite components need harmony. The butter must blend with the flour. The eggs must temper into the custard. Likewise, in the supply chain, your internal capabilities are only as powerful as the relationships you build outside your own walls. That means it's time to turn our focus from the kitchen to the market—from what's in your hands to who's shaking yours.

Next, we'll roll up our sleeves and begin whisking the next essential ingredient: **supplier relationships**. Because behind every perfect dish—whether it's a plated microchip or a seared duck breast—is a network of farmers, foragers, and vendors. The trick isn't just finding the right ingredients; it's partnering with those who know how to grow, deliver, and evolve with you.

So, tighten your apron. We're stepping out of the prep zone and into the heart of collaboration.

It's time to make some culinary connections.

2

WHISKING INGREDIENTS – SUPPLIER RELATIONSHIPS

Selecting the Right Ingredients – Finding Suppliers Who Make the Dish Sing

IN THE WORLD of supply chain management, much like the bustling back kitchen of a Michelin-starred restaurant, the magic doesn't just lie in the ingredients—it lies in the relationships. While the menu may boast exquisite delicacies and the plating may dazzle, the real alchemy begins with the suppliers—the unsung heroes delivering crates of potential. In our case, these crates contain semiconductor-grade silicon, copper foils, specialty gases, or micro-components so precise they make a soufflé look forgiving. If a chef's success hinges on trusted purveyors, then a supply chain's resilience is cooked into the strength of its supplier network.

Let's start with the supplier scene from a chef's lens. Imagine walking through a farmer's market. Each vendor has a story. The tomato farmer might speak passionately about his heirlooms while offering samples still warm from the sun. The fishmonger knows exactly when the catch landed and why today's yellowtail sings with freshness. Similarly, in semiconductor supply chains, each supplier holds unique capabilities, constraints, and context. It's not just about who gives the best quote—

it's about understanding what drives their reliability, how they mitigate risk, and whether they'll deliver your high-spec fluoropolymer under duress. Like a chef developing rapport with the forager who brings rare mushrooms, procurement professionals must build layered relationships that go beyond RFPs.

Let's also talk about communication—seasoned, not sugarcoated. A great supplier won't always tell you what you want to hear, but they'll tell you what you need to know. Think of a chef's trusted butcher who flags, "Hey, your wagyu's marbling isn't up to scratch today—try the rib cap instead." In our world, that might sound like, "Our lead time just slipped by two weeks due to helium shortages—but here's a mitigation plan." Transparency is the spice that prevents bitter surprises. Case in point: when a critical raw material for photoresist chemicals was hit by upstream contamination in Japan, long-time suppliers who proactively communicated and collaborated on inventory buffering saved fabs from halts. That level of trust is like knowing your oven's exact hot spots.

Negotiation, too, is part of the kitchen dance. But here, it's not about strong-arming vendors into discounts; it's about value creation. Can your supplier offer lot traceability down to the mine source? Are they willing to co-invest in capacity or expedite tooling for a new node transition? One global packaging site in Malaysia turned a standard capex delay into a co-funded tooling upgrade with their supplier, saving time and cost—think of it like a pastry chef receiving an upgraded mixer gratis because they had always paid invoices early and beta-tested new designs. That's the kind of supplier loyalty money can't buy.

Then there's the art of adapting. When a preferred graphite carrier vendor was flooded during monsoon season, a nimble global commodity manager (yes, yours truly) activated an alternate partner in South Korea within days—thanks to years of supplier scorecarding, backup qualification runs, and ongoing "pastry tastings" (a.k.a. informal trust-building lunches). This wasn't luck; it was mise en place for a crisis.

Lastly, let's not ignore flavor. Differentiation lies in collaboration. Want exclusive plating? Co-design your components. Host quarterly innovation forums. Invite your suppliers to walk the production line and help you spot upstream tweaks. Just as chefs partner with vineyards to create house wines, we must empower suppliers to become more than providers—they become creators. Together, we're not just filling orders; we're crafting recipes for long-term competitive advantage.

In short, supplier relationships are the aromatic base stock in our supply chain kitchen. Build them with patience, consistency, and a little creative spice, and you'll never serve up bland results. Ready your whisk—we're just getting started.

Whisking Up Trust - Building Strong Relationships

In the kitchen and in the global supply chain, trust is the invisible ingredient that binds every successful recipe. It's what keeps a soufflé from collapsing when the heat rises—and what ensures a supplier delivers even when the market is boiling over. Building strong supplier relationships isn't a garnish to your strategy; it's the roux that holds your operation together.

Start with transparency. Like a chef tasting every sauce before plating, you must know what's really going into your supply chain. A supplier who sugarcoats delays or downplays risks is like a sous-chef hiding overcooked duck breast beneath garnish. Trust is built when suppliers are upfront—when they proactively alert you to yield issues in the fab, changes in raw material specs, or labor shortages that could snowball into shipment delays. In return, transparency must be mutual. Share your forecast. Explain the rationale behind your scorecarding. Open your kitchen and let them see the menu for next quarter's big launch.

Consistency is next. Just as guests return for that one perfect dish made flawlessly every time, your suppliers must feel that your expectations, payment cycles, and communication cadence are dependable. That's why regular check-ins—weekly, monthly, or quarterly—are vital. Whether through QBRs, site visits, or joint innovation reviews, these moments are the stirring spoon in the pot, keeping the flavors evenly blended. I once flew to a supplier's headquarters in Austria for a midwinter planning review. The result? They rerouted a critical shipment that same week, saving my fab from a painful shutdown. That wasn't about logistics; it was about loyalty.

Then comes the seasoning: recognition and respect. A handwritten thank-you after a successful product launch. A call-out during a town hall. A social media post spotlighting a partner's contribution. These are the herbs and spices of rapport. I've seen suppliers go the extra mile after a simple box of cookies showed up with a note that read, "You saved our Q1." Simple gestures, baked in sincerity, often yield the richest returns.

Also critical: navigating conflict like a chef de cuisine handles a kitchen meltdown—with composure and candor. When a materials lot failed inspection and tensions ran high, I invited the supplier's quality manager to our site, rolled up my sleeves, and walked the floor together. We solved the root issue, reinforced specs, and redesigned the shipment protocol. What could've been a scorched-earth episode became a masterclass in collaboration.

Lastly, build in flexibility. Your supplier today may be your innovation partner tomorrow. Offer joint workshops. Support their continuous improvement efforts. Help them grow as you grow. It's the culinary equivalent of nurturing a line cook into a sous-chef—elevating the whole brigade.

Strong supplier relationships don't just help you weather storms—they make your supply chain stormproof. So, whip up those bonds with authenticity, and don't be afraid to serve up a little heart along the way.

The Supplier Pantry – Segmenting for Strategic Flavor

A master chef doesn't toss all ingredients into one bowl without thought—and neither should you treat every supplier the same. Just as the pantry in a fine kitchen separates spices, proteins, and perishables based on their roles and handling requirements, supply chains must strategically segment suppliers to extract the best value and performance from each relationship. Supplier segmentation is the art of understanding who brings what to the table and tailoring engagement accordingly.

Think of your supplier base as a stocked pantry: your premium innovation partners are like truffles and saffron—rare, high-touch, and mission-critical. They require close collaboration, long-term contracts, and constant dialogue. At the other end, transactional suppliers are your staples—salt, sugar, and flour. Reliable, bulk-order players who deliver consistent inputs but don't require constant oversight. Then there are strategic enablers—your herbs and specialty oils—who enhance the recipe in unique ways and offer niche capabilities. Segmenting suppliers this way lets you allocate your time, energy, and negotiation tactics wisely.

In semiconductor manufacturing, the benefits of segmentation are tangible. For instance, a large fab in Arizona categorized its materials suppliers into four tiers: strategic, preferred, qualified, and transactional. This approach allowed procurement to identify which partners deserved co-location in their R&D labs, which needed quarterly business reviews, and which could be managed via digital portals. When a rare earth metal shortage disrupted the availability of yttrium oxide (a material used in CVD chamber coatings), the fab prioritized communication with its Tier 1 partner, who had early visibility into the crisis and locked in allocation proactively. Meanwhile, low-tier suppliers were simply put on pause, freeing bandwidth to manage what mattered most.

Segmentation also enhances resilience. During the COVID-19 pandemic, a major packaging house in Southeast Asia segmented its PPE and chemical suppliers to isolate risks. High-touch vendors received direct updates, while a pool of interchangeable providers was prequalified for fast substitution. This strategy kept the cleanroom stocked and the production line humming while others scrambled.

Don't underestimate the power of internal alignment, either. Sharing your supplier segmentation framework across engineering, operations, and finance ensures a unified approach to engagement. After all, your pastry chef shouldn't be placing orders for truffle oil behind the executive chef's back. A shared supplier strategy streamlines onboarding, performance reviews, and even escalation protocols.

So grab a label maker—or better yet, a scorecard—and start segmenting. By organizing your supplier pantry, you'll reduce chaos, improve decision-making, and know exactly where to reach when the next culinary challenge strikes. The result? A supply chain that cooks with precision, poise, and purpose.

Joint Menu Development - Co-Innovation at the Supplier Table

Innovation doesn't happen in a vacuum—or in a lonely kitchen. Often, the next big idea is born not in a corporate R&D lab but over a shared espresso with a supplier who knows your recipe better than anyone. Just as visionary chefs co-create signature dishes with local producers and artisans, supply chain leaders must invite suppliers into the innovation tent. When done right, co-innovation isn't just efficient—it's delicious.

Consider the case of a Japanese semiconductor OEM that was transitioning to a more energy-efficient etching process. Instead of simply specifying a new component and tossing the challenge over the fence, they invited their supplier—an advanced materials firm from Belgium—to co-develop a new coating chemistry. The result wasn't just a product that met specifications; it was a process breakthrough that cut tool downtime by 12% and earned both parties a joint patent.

This kind of magic starts with early engagement. Bring suppliers into your roadmap discussions, even at the pre-concept phase. Share your challenges like a chef describing an elusive flavor profile. Be honest: "We're trying to improve deposition uniformity at lower temps without sacrificing throughput—can we build a better whisk together?" You'd be amazed at how often suppliers have R&D assets and ideas simmering on the back burner, waiting for a strategic partner to spark them into flame.

To cultivate this spirit, build joint development agreements (JDAs), non-disclosure frameworks, and milestone incentives. Consider hosting a "Supplier Innovation Day" where teams pitch wild ideas, much like a test kitchen's tasting menu trial. I've seen vendors surprise even the most skeptical engineers with low-cost thermal control modules developed in-house using automotive-grade logic—a cross-industry infusion that would have been missed without intentional collaboration.

But co-innovation isn't all rainbows and reductions. You must align on IP ownership, data security, and mutual goals. Set clear check-in milestones. Keep the heat manageable so your ideas don't curdle under pressure. And when the partnership bears fruit, celebrate it together. Co-branding a success, submitting a joint industry award, or even writing a white paper can amplify both parties' reputations.

In short, don't just give your suppliers a recipe—invite them to write it with you. Because when you co-develop the menu, you don't just improve your product; you cultivate a relationship rich in trust, technical depth, and creative joy. And that's a taste that lingers.

Keeping the Kitchen Clean - Ethics, Compliance, and Responsible Sourcing

Any chef worth their salt knows that cleanliness is non-negotiable. You can have the finest ingredients, but if your prep station is a mess, you're cooking up trouble. Similarly, in supply chain management, ethics and compliance are the hygiene practices that prevent contamination, crisis, and reputational indigestion. Responsible sourcing isn't just a checkbox—it's the baseline for culinary excellence.

In semiconductor manufacturing, where the upstream web of suppliers spans continents and conflict zones, transparency is vital. Minerals like tantalum, tungsten, and cobalt—essential for chip production—have historically been linked to human rights abuses in mining. That's why industry giants like Intel and Apple have invested heavily in conflict mineral tracking and smelter verification. Their message? "We won't build tomorrow's technology on yesterday's exploitation."

Responsible sourcing starts with a clear Supplier Code of Conduct. This is your "kitchen hygiene checklist"—covering labor standards, environmental practices, anti-bribery rules, and more. Make it visible. Train on it. Audit to it. One site I worked with in Malaysia incorporated its ethical sourcing clause directly into tooling RFQs and awarded bonus points for ISO 14001 and SA8000 compliance. It didn't just raise the bar; it filtered out suppliers who didn't belong in a clean kitchen.

But policies alone won't keep the pot from boiling over. Active monitoring and tier-2 visibility are essential. If your Tier 1 supplier sources rare earths from a sub-supplier in Inner Mongolia, you need to know. Are they compliant? Are they safe? Do they pay their workers fairly and manage waste responsibly? It's like checking the kitchen's back door—what's coming in could affect everything going out.

Technology can help. Platforms like Sourcemap and Assent offer digital supply chain mapping tools that track ESG risks from mine to module. Consider implementing these as part of your supplier onboarding or quarterly reviews. And when in doubt, do a surprise audit—the corporate equivalent of a "white glove" inspection.

Responsible sourcing also drives resilience. When COVID hit, suppliers with strong labor practices and health protocols rebounded faster. When new EU sustainability directives roll out, those already aligned will remain eligible vendors. Ethics isn't just about doing good—it's about being ready.

In the end, a clean kitchen isn't just a point of pride—it's what keeps customers safe, regulators at bay, and your conscience clear. So put on your apron, grab the clipboard, and commit to sourcing that's as pure as your intentions. Your supply chain—and your stakeholders—will thank you.

3

THE MISE EN PLACE - PREPARATION IS KEY

Organizing Resources: Essential Tools and Proven Techniques

YOU WOULDN'T WALK into a kitchen and expect to whip up a ten-course tasting menu without your mise en place—so why would you manage a global supply chain without your tools, systems, and teams prepped and organized? Just as a chef's success hinges on having the right knife, a sharp peeler, and a perfectly sorted spice rack, the health of your supply chain depends on how well you've organized your resources. Because when the heat rises—and it always does—you'll want everything within reach and ready to go.

Think of organizing resources as designing your supply chain's prep station. It's about more than just having the right stuff—it's about having it accessible, visible, and usable at the moment it's needed. That means your digital systems, data streams, supplier contacts, inventory levels, and cross-functional workflows must operate like a top-tier kitchen brigade: fast, seamless, and fully aligned.

Let's start with technology—the sous-chef that never sleeps. In semiconductor manufacturing, tools like ERP (Enterprise Resource Planning), SCM (Supply Chain Management), and MES

(Manufacturing Execution Systems) are as fundamental as a food processor in a commercial kitchen. They handle the slicing, dicing, blending, and timing behind the scenes. For example, a fab in Korea leveraged SAP's Integrated Business Planning (IBP) to integrate demand forecasts with supply scenarios, which helped them rebalance wafer starts within 12 hours of a major customer pull-in. No flailing, no fire—just a well-choreographed pivot.

Then there's the power of visibility. Cloud-based platforms like Kinaxis Rapid Response and Oracle SCM Cloud give supply chain managers a live view of inventory, supplier status, logistics, and capacity. It's the equivalent of a prep chef who doesn't just chop vegetables but color-codes them by freshness, allergen level, and meal plan priority. When one plant in Taiwan faced a material shortage, the digital twin flagged the constraint before it impacted builds—giving the team enough time to substitute parts without halting the line.

Of course, tools are nothing without the people who wield them. Just like in a kitchen, you need trained hands behind every piece of equipment. Building capability around digital systems and empowering your team to act on data insights is crucial. I once visited a packaging site in the Philippines where procurement analysts were trained not just in spreadsheets but in scenario modeling. When a typhoon delayed inbound chemicals, their team rerouted suppliers, prioritized critical batches, and still hit the monthly yield target. That's the power of preparation.

Let's also talk about standard work and SOPs—the laminated recipe cards of the supply chain world. Having playbooks for demand changes, supplier escalations, and factory loading scenarios ensures your team doesn't have to reinvent the wheel under pressure. These documents serve the same purpose as the notes chefs scribble in the margins: hard-won wisdom that saves time and avoids disaster.

And just like every good kitchen has a walk-in fridge with inventory clearly labeled and rotated, your supply chain should have robust inventory control. Kanban systems, cycle counts, and safety stock policies prevent both spoilage and starvation. One advanced node operation in Oregon used RFID tagging to track critical consumables. When a sudden spike in oxide liner demand occurred, they were able to identify exactly which bins needed restocking—and which were overstocked. No waste. No guesswork. Just precision.

Let's not forget communication tools. Whether it's Slack, Teams, or a good old-fashioned war room whiteboard, clear, timely updates can mean the difference between a controlled recovery and a full-on service failure. I've seen supplier escalation meetings run like kitchen line checks: quick, specific, and solutions-focused. Keep it brief, keep it sharp, and keep the stove hot.

So, before you chase that next big initiative, ask yourself: Is your kitchen ready? Are your tools clean, your people trained, your processes mapped, and your dashboards lit up like a heat lamp over a plated entrée? Because in supply chain—as in the kitchen—flavor follows function. Get your mise en place right, and you'll be serving up excellence every time the dinner bell rings.

Forecasting Demand: The Key Ingredient

Forecasting demand—the mystical art that turns data, intuition, and timing into a five-star recipe for operational success. Just as a chef anticipates the number of guests for dinner service, a supply chain manager must predict customer needs before the first wafer even touches the production line. Miss the mark, and you're either stuck with empty plates or food going cold. Hit it just right, and you orchestrate a flawless flow from raw materials to customer satisfaction.

In the semiconductor world, demand forecasting is less about crystal balls and more about dynamic modeling. Picture this: a fab preparing for a product ramp on a node still in customer qualification. You don't just guess volumes—you model customer pull scenarios, lead times, risk buffers, and end-market signals. It's like prepping mise en place not just for today's dinner rush, but also for tomorrow's private tasting event and next week's pop-up. Smart forecasting helps you balance capacity and risk with just the right dash of flexibility.

A U.S.-based substrate supplier once avoided a multimillion-dollar stockout by integrating its sales pipeline with customer tool install timelines. This foresight allowed it to pre-position high-demand SKUs near customer sites in Malaysia, shaving down lead times and turning reactive firefighting into proactive service. That's forecasting done right—it doesn't just inform; it empowers.

But forecasting isn't all spreadsheets and dashboards. It's a blend of structured analytics and gut feel—what I like to call "data-seasoned intuition." Take the 2020 surge in notebook demand when remote work took off. Many supply chain teams dismissed the initial spike as a blip. But the savvy ones—those with ears to the market, vendor signals, and even retail trends—pivoted early. They leaned into the buildup, secured capacity, and captured market share.

Tools like machine learning, AI-driven demand planning, and predictive analytics platforms (like Blue Yonder or SAS) can detect patterns humans might miss. But they shine brightest when paired with domain expertise. After all, knowing when to trust the model—and when to override it based on what's brewing in customer discussions—is a skill honed over time.

Another key ingredient? Cross-functional collaboration. Just as kitchen staff must align on plating times, flavor profiles, and order sequence, supply chain teams need synchronized forecasts from sales, marketing, finance, and ops. Sales might forecast optimism, finance demands realism, and manufacturing wants clarity. Reconciling these perspectives is what transforms fragmented guesses into a cohesive plan.

And don't forget external signals. Market trends, competitor launches, geopolitical events—they're the ambient temperature in your kitchen. Are customers ramping up AI-enabled devices? Are export restrictions looming? Is there a whisper of M&A in the air? Monitoring these cues ensures your forecast isn't operating in a vacuum.

The best forecasters also know when not to overcommit. They build flexibility into their models, creating scenarios that prepare for best-case, worst-case, and "didn't-see-that-coming" outcomes. This mindset

—of building range, not just precision—helps teams stay agile without flipping the whole soufflé.

In the end, forecasting is both an art and a science. It's the intuitive timing of pulling a roast from the oven when it's just right—not overcooked, not raw. In your supply chain kitchen, that intuition—backed by data, technology, and teamwork—is the key to serving what your customers need, when they need it.

So sharpen your knives, clear your dashboards, and gather your team. Forecasting isn't just a planning exercise—it's the first step in delighting your customer. Bon appétit!

The Kitchen Clock: Mastering Timing and Flow

In any world-class kitchen, timing is the unsung hero behind every perfectly plated dish. It's the difference between golden, crispy perfection and something that ends up in the compost bin. And in the supply chain—especially in high-mix, high-stakes environments like semiconductors—timing isn't just important; it's everything. Whether you're sourcing rare components, orchestrating global logistics, or lining up production steps, flow matters. The clock is ticking, and every second counts.

Let's start with the basics: flow. In the culinary world, this means understanding how each station—prep, sauté, grill, pastry—connects to the next. In supply chain terms, it's the synchronized movement of materials, data, and decisions across functions. When flow is optimized, there's no idle time, no bottlenecks, and no one shouting, "Where's the sauce?!" during service. Instead, it's a smooth, orchestrated rhythm that allows throughput to hum like a well-tuned oven fan.

One real-world example? A chip packaging site in Taiwan redesigned its production line using lean flow principles—similar to reconfiguring a cramped kitchen to improve the cook's reach. By adjusting workstation layout and implementing real-time WIP visibility via overhead screens, they reduced handoff delays by 30%

and shortened build cycles by nearly two days. Faster plating, better reviews.

Now let's talk about takt time—the heartbeat of any production line. Takt time tells you how fast you need to produce to meet customer demand. If the kitchen gets an order every three minutes, your cooks better serve every three minutes—or risk hangry customers. Similarly, if your customer wants 1,000 die-attached components per day, your takt must match that drumbeat. Too fast, and you overproduce; too slow, and your backlog builds up like a line out the door.

To master timing, you also need lead time intelligence. Think of lead time like marinating: some tasks just take time. If your substrates take 10 weeks to arrive, you can't start cooking the day before the dinner party. You plan ahead, you sequence, and you buffer where needed. At one OSAT (Outsourced Semiconductor Assembly & Testing) partner site, a vendor-managed inventory model was implemented for ceramic packages with volatile demand. By pre-positioning materials based on forecasted takt and aligning transit lead time, they cut expedite costs in half and improved service levels.

But beware the seductive danger of over-buffering. Stockpiling "just in case" is like prepping three of every dish before orders are placed—wasteful, inefficient, and eventually a logistical nightmare. Flow isn't about hoarding; it's about trust in timing. Smart kitchens and smart supply chains rely on systems like Kanban, pull signals, and exception-based triggers to move inventory only when needed. It's supply chain mise en place in motion.

Digitization is your secret weapon. Digital control towers, MES dashboards, and AI-based ETA predictors are like the expo chef who oversees the whole kitchen, calling out when dishes need to fire and when they hit the pass. A semiconductor firm in Oregon deployed an AI engine linked to its shop floor data and vendor lead times. The result? An 11% reduction in line changeover time and 95% on-time delivery—even through seasonal volatility. That's the kind of timing that earns five-star reviews.

And then there's human flow—labor choreography. A kitchen only works if the sauté chef doesn't step over the pastry chef and spill the béchamel. Cross-training, shift balancing, and team huddles ensure smooth handoffs and fewer missteps. One Southeast Asia assembly site created a "flow coach" role—think "maître d'" meets industrial engineer—to ensure operators, tools, and materials moved in sync. The result? Fewer idle tools, better morale, and yes, more productivity.

At the end of the day, mastering timing and flow isn't about micromanagement—it's about trust, visibility, and discipline. When your systems pulse in harmony, your supply chain becomes agile, responsive, and resilient. It can take the heat. It can scale the recipe. And it can keep customers coming back for more.

So cue the timers, light the burners, and get your brigade in sync. In the kitchen of supply chain, mastering timing and flow is what separates a slammed service from a standing ovation.

Cross-Training Your Kitchen Crew: Building Agility into Your Workforce

In a Michelin-starred kitchen, there's an unspoken rule: everyone should be able to jump in wherever needed. If the pastry chef suddenly calls out, the sous chef better know how to torch a crème brûlée without turning it into carbon. That kind of flexibility isn't just culinary wizardry—it's workforce agility. And in the supply chain, especially in industries as fast-paced as semiconductors, cross-training is the "secret sauce" that keeps the whole operation from boiling over.

Cross-training your supply chain team is like seasoning your crew with a blend of skills that allows them to move between roles, troubleshoot bottlenecks, and adapt to shifting priorities without missing a beat. Imagine a planner who understands procurement lead times or a buyer who knows how production schedules are sequenced. That knowledge isn't just nice to have—it's transformational.

Take, for example, a chip assembly site in Penang. During a surge in demand for high-bandwidth memory components, the team faced a backlog in inbound logistics. Rather than grind operations to a halt, cross-trained material handlers from the warehouse stepped in to support the planning team. Within a week, they cleared the backlog and re-sequenced builds without a single missed ship date. It was a bit like the dishwasher grabbing a sauté pan and pulling off a perfect risotto—unexpected, efficient, and heroic.

But cross-training isn't just a crisis tool; it builds resilience. When employees are trained across functions, the organization becomes less vulnerable to turnover, vacation gaps, or sudden demand shifts. It's a buffer against the unknown—like having backup knives when your favorite one goes missing mid-service.

Structured job rotation programs can help bake this into your team's development. Think of it like a culinary apprenticeship where staff spend time in every station: from sourcing and planning to logistics and fulfillment. Not only does this deepen their operational understanding, but it fosters empathy across departments and minimizes the "us vs. them" dynamic that can brew when teams operate in silos.

Technology can help, too. Digital playbooks, SOP libraries, and on-demand training modules allow employees to pick up new roles without waiting for a formal class. At one European OSAT provider, a cross-functional knowledge base built in Notion helped new hires ramp up 40% faster—and even seasoned staff used it to refresh their skills before rotation assignments.

Cross-training also enhances engagement. When people grow, they stay. When they feel confident jumping into new roles, they bring new ideas to the table. One planner in Arizona who rotated through a logistics role suggested rerouting carrier lanes based on cycle time data she had learned to interpret—saving $60K in just one quarter.

And finally, it's about culture. Cross-training sends a clear message: we are one kitchen, one team. Everyone shares responsibility for the meal—and the mission. That mindset? It turns cooks into collaborators and workers into owners. And that's when the magic happens.

So if your supply chain is feeling stretched, stale, or just plain sluggish, consider stirring in a little cross-training. Like a versatile kitchen crew, an agile team can cook up success no matter what ingredients the day throws at them.

Mise en Place Meets Murphy's Law: Planning for the Unexpected

Even in the most meticulously organized kitchens, something always burns, breaks, or simply doesn't show up. The same goes for supply chains. You can have a beautifully aligned demand forecast, a fully trained team, and digital dashboards glowing like a hot pass—and still get sideswiped by the unexpected: a late shipment, a customs delay, or a machine breakdown. Enter the art of planning for the unplanned.

In culinary terms, this is your backup mise en place. Think of a seasoned chef who doesn't just prep ingredients for the menu but also keeps a spare sauce, backup protein, or an off-menu special ready in case of disaster. In the supply chain world, it's the principle of operational buffers and contingency frameworks designed not to slow you down but to let you recover faster when the burners blow out.

Contingency menus can take many forms: dual sourcing, pre-approved alternates, and regionally distributed suppliers that act as redundancies when geopolitical risks or natural disasters strike. A sourcing manager in Austin, Texas, once shared how their team prequalified a secondary epoxy vendor across the Pacific—so when a major resin supplier faced an unplanned outage, they activated the contingency supplier and kept wafer production running smoothly.

Scenario planning and digital twins serve as prep lists for potential disasters. Just as chefs visualize the worst-case scenarios during a busy shift—a power outage, a spoiled delivery—supply chain professionals can model disruptions and rehearse reactions. Tools like AnyLogic or SAP's Supply Chain Control Tower can simulate ripple effects across the network, helping you choose which fires to extinguish first.

Some organizations even go a step further by pre-staging inventory in virtual warehouses. Think of this as storing your dessert course on a rolling cart in the hallway—close enough to access when needed, but out of the way until the time comes. These virtual buffers can be unlocked when disruptions delay primary shipments. A fabless chip designer once used bonded inventory hubs in Singapore to manage volatile memory component needs, activating them only when Asian ports were gridlocked.

And let's not forget about having clearly defined, practiced SOPs for crisis response. A laminated recipe card won't save your soufflé if no one knows how to turn off the oven. Regular dry runs, tabletop exercises, and scenario walkthroughs can ensure that when disruption strikes, the team doesn't just panic—they perform.

Planning for the unexpected isn't about fear—it's about resilience. The kitchen will heat up. Something will go wrong. The question is: Are you ready to improvise, adapt, and deliver a delicious outcome anyway? When your mise en place includes a backup plan, your team can handle anything the dinner rush—or the supply chain—throws at them.

Finishing the Prep: From Chopped to Chef'd

As the chapter draws to a close, we come back to where we began: the kitchen before service. Everything we've covered—forecasting demand, aligning resources, mastering timing, cultivating agility, and planning for curveballs—is about one thing: readiness. Preparation is the bridge between chaos and control, the secret that transforms a flustered back room into a place of precision, rhythm, and pride.

Whether you're scaling up production at a new OSAT facility or rolling out a product ramp in three global regions, the principles remain the same: prep what you can and build in room to breathe. Know your tools, train your crew, and anticipate that something will go wrong—but you'll be ready.

In the next chapter, we move from preparation to execution. Because just as a mise en place means nothing if the dish isn't cooked to order, your careful planning only comes alive when you start "Timing the Bake." So sharpen those knives and preheat your ovens—it's go time.

4

TIMING THE BAKE - SYNCHRONIZING SUPPLY AND DEMAND

When Orders Overflow - Managing Demand Volatility Without Boiling Over

EVERY CHEF KNOWS the moment when a calm kitchen suddenly shifts into frenzy: tickets printing nonstop, the fryer at full tilt, soufflés queued in the oven. In the supply chain world, this same energy arrives in the form of demand volatility—sudden surges, shifts, or stalls that can overwhelm even the most finely tuned operation.

In semiconductors, volatility isn't a rare disruption; it's a constant companion. One quarter might bring an unexpected AI boom that consumes every available substrate, while the next sees consumer electronics softening, leaving shelves full of unsold stock. Like steam rising from a pan, demand moves quickly, unpredictably, and with the potential to scald if you're unprepared.

Managing these swings requires agility rather than rigidity. Just as a smart chef preps mise en place for a range of dishes, a resilient supply chain builds flexibility into planning, procurement, and production. One fab-lite company in South Korea adopted dual sourcing with mirrored suppliers in Taiwan. When a surge threatened to choke their primary partner, the second was already qualified and ready—like having a backup soufflé in a second oven.

But volatility isn't only about floods of orders; sometimes it's about sudden droughts. Over-forecasting can leave inventory piled like overstocked pantries, tying up capital and morale. Under-forecasting starves the line and risks customers walking away hungry. Balancing these extremes requires visibility and discipline. Predictive analytics, AI demand sensing, and digital control towers act like seasoned expeditors, scanning the dining room and signaling when to fire the next course. A European chip distributor used demand-sensing tools to cut expedite costs by 40%, smoothing swings that would have crippled operations only a few years earlier.

Still, technology alone can't tame volatility. It takes strong cross-functional alignment. Sales must share forecasts candidly, operations must flag real capacity limits, and finance must weigh risk trade-offs. One analog device manufacturer instituted "Flash S&OP" sessions—emergency huddles when anomalies exceeded set thresholds. Like a head chef calling the brigade together mid-service, these quick stand-ups let the team pivot before chaos consumed the floor.

Ultimately, volatility will never vanish. Customers will surge unexpectedly; markets will cool without warning. The goal isn't to outlaw unpredictability but to build a supply chain that flexes, absorbs, and recovers without compromising quality or burning out resources. Just as diners return to a restaurant that handles a rush with grace, customers trust suppliers who can absorb market swings without missing a beat.

In the end, managing demand volatility isn't about perfection. It's about resilience—the ability to keep the kitchen humming, whether tickets flood in or tables sit empty. A supply chain that can ride those waves with confidence earns not just efficiency, but loyalty that lasts.

Too Many Cooks - Taming Complexity in the Global Kitchen

There's an old kitchen saying: "Too many cooks spoil the broth." But in today's global supply chains—especially in the semiconductor world—it's more like, "Too many SKUs, partners, exceptions, and regions spoil the flow." Complexity is the uninvited sous chef that sneaks into your kitchen, makes everything harder to clean, and throws off your timing. It's subtle, persistent, and, if left unchecked, can burn your entire operation.

Complexity shows up in all kinds of disguises: a growing number of customer configurations, country-specific compliance, dual-redundant suppliers, or that one assembly line that still runs on software from the Jurassic era. And while complexity is often born from good intentions—more options for customers, more flexibility for sourcing—it rarely arrives without a cost. Just ask any chef who's tried to plate twelve different entrées for a table of six.

In the semiconductor industry, complexity is particularly sticky. With product life cycles shrinking, end-user demand spiking unpredictably, and geographic constraints impacting raw material sourcing, managing the moving pieces can feel like sautéing onions, flipping fish, and flambéing dessert—all at once, with one hand tied behind your back.

One fab in South Korea tackled this head-on by mapping out every production flow variation across its product families. The result? Over 120 unique build recipes—each with its own routing, toolsets, and supplier constraints. By categorizing them into "core," "variable," and "niche," the team was able to reduce their active configurations by 40%, simplify their MRP logic, and stabilize their yield performance. Like simplifying a menu to focus on signature dishes, this cut through the noise and improved customer lead times.

Another technique is **modularization**—designing components or processes that can be easily swapped or reused. Think of it like prepping a base sauce that works for pasta, rice, or protein. One IDM (Integrated Design Manufacturer) launched a modular test socket program across its backend test sites. By standardizing interfaces and allowing rapid configuration changes, it reduced NPI test setup time by 60%. Simpler parts, faster plating.

Complexity doesn't just burden operations—it chokes visibility. The more steps, the greater the chance for a handoff to break. That's why smart supply chains invest in end-to-end digital thread visibility. A major EMS provider adopted a centralized BOM management system linked to their MES, supplier portals, and demand forecast engines. The result? Fewer miscommunications, faster ECO turnarounds, and far less time spent chasing parts that don't exist.

But here's the trick—taming complexity isn't about eliminating variety. It's about **managing it with intention**. Every dish on the menu should have a purpose, just like every SKU or process path in your network. If it doesn't add customer value or operational flexibility, it's just adding noise.

So, ask yourself: Is this configuration essential, or just habitual? Is this supplier truly strategic, or just a leftover from a past program? When you pare down to what matters, you can plate faster, serve smarter, and scale without feeling like the kitchen is on fire.

Clear View, Clean Plate - Achieving End-to-End Visibility

Imagine trying to cook a five-course meal... blindfolded. You don't know what's been prepped, what's still cooking, or if the server has already picked up the salad. That's what it feels like to run a supply chain without visibility. You might have all the right ingredients, the best tools, and the finest chefs—but without the ability to see across the kitchen, things unravel quickly.

In supply chain management—particularly in the complex, multi-layered world of semiconductors—visibility is the flame beneath the stove. It's not just about knowing where your parts are; it's about understanding where everything is and where it's going. It's about connecting your supply network like a mise en place spread across the globe: clear, organized, and accessible in real time.

Consider this: a fabless chipmaker in California once dealt with a chronic problem—line stoppages due to a single passive component consistently arriving late from Asia. The root cause? A third-tier sub-supplier delay, completely invisible to the Tier 1 partner. After implementing a supply chain control tower solution that integrated data from contract manufacturers, logistics partners, and upstream raw material vendors, they reduced surprise shortages by 60% and cut unplanned expediting costs by over $2 million annually. Visibility turned "firefighting" into "foresight."

Control towers, digital twins, and integrated dashboards are more than buzzwords—they're the new "kitchen pass." These tools offer dynamic views of inventory, production status, supplier performance, and customer demand. You can see what's hot, what's held up, and what's about to boil over. Better still, they can simulate scenarios—so when a critical shipment is stuck in customs or a tool goes down, you can instantly reroute the recipe without overcooking the whole order.

Think of real-time tracking as your sous chef calling out the status of every dish: "Table 6, mains ready! Table 2, dessert plating in 2!" When every part of your supply chain can call and respond with precision, you don't just react—you orchestrate. That's the difference between chaos and cadence.

End-to-end visibility also builds trust. When teams across procurement, logistics, finance, and sales see the same dashboard, the finger-pointing stops. Everyone operates from a single source of truth—less guesswork, fewer escalations, and more proactive planning. One OSAT in Penang introduced a cross-functional visibility board for WIP and material status. Suddenly, the weekly meetings shifted from blame games to solution sessions.

But visibility is only as strong as its weakest data source. If your systems are siloed, your vendors guarded, or your updates lag by days, your line of sight is clouded. Clean data, integrated systems, and supplier collaboration are the essential seasonings here—without them, you're cooking with the lights off.

So, what's the takeaway? You can't optimize what you can't see. Whether it's a missing component, a misaligned forecast, or a mounting backlog, clarity gives you control. And in the fast-paced world of silicon, a clear line of sight can mean the difference between sizzling success and a supply chain soufflé that falls flat.

Smart Sequencing - Plating the Right Dish at the Right Time

Every chef knows there's an art to timing—not just when to cook a dish, but which dish to cook first. You don't start the risotto when the steak hits the pan, and you certainly don't fire dessert while the appetizers are still at the pass. It's a choreography, a dance of preparation and execution—sequencing that ensures everything lands perfectly on the plate, at the right temperature, and at the right time.

In the supply chain kitchen—particularly in semiconductor manufacturing, where tool utilization, cleanroom flow, and queue times are critical—smart sequencing plays the same role. It's the difference between a smooth production line and a tangled web of half-cooked orders.

Think of it like this: sequencing is your kitchen's ticket system. It decides which orders go first, which can wait, and which need to be expedited because someone's birthday cake (or, in our case, a top customer's eval tool) just became a red-alert priority.

A compelling example comes from a backend assembly site in the Philippines. Struggling with high WIP levels and extended cycle times, they restructured their production sequence logic using constraint-based scheduling. By prioritizing high-mix, low-volume builds based on delivery urgency, material readiness, and test line availability, they reduced cycle times by 18% and achieved a 30% improvement in on-time delivery. That's not just plating efficiency—it's customer satisfaction on a silver tray.

In supply chain terms, sequencing decisions are often guided by rules-based engines, advanced planning systems, or AI algorithms that analyze multiple variables: lead times, setup costs, batch sizes, labor availability, and customer SLAs. The goal? Minimize idle tools, reduce changeovers, and maximize throughput—just like a kitchen trying to keep every burner cooking without anything burning.

Let's bring in a semiconductor-specific example. At a wafer sort facility in Texas, engineers implemented dynamic dispatching logic integrated into their MES. The system assessed each lot's customer priority, tool readiness, and next operation before assigning it a run slot. This adaptive sequence cut lot wait time by 22% and eliminated Friday night scrambles to meet quarter-end shipments. Fewer heroics. More consistency. And fewer burnt soufflés at the finish line.

Smart sequencing is also about communication. In kitchens, the expo coordinates the line—"Fire table 12's entrée in 3 minutes!" The supply chain needs the same clarity: planners, operators, and logistics teams all working from one synchronized priority list. Tools like SAP PPDS or Kinaxis scenarios help teams model the impact of sequence changes before a single part is touched—because no one likes remaking an order mid-service.

But sequencing isn't just about speed—it's about alignment. If upstream suppliers are running behind, there's no use in pulling forward a build that will sit incomplete. Smart sequencing adapts to the reality of available ingredients and kitchen constraints, keeping the meal on track, even when the delivery truck is late.

In short, the perfect plate is as much about when it's cooked as how. In the world of high-tech manufacturing and global logistics, smart sequencing ensures your operations aren't just busy—they're beautifully timed. It's not just about working harder; it's about cooking smarter.

Demand Shaping - Influencing the Order Before It's Placed

Before a single pan hits the stove or a single part enters production, there's a moment of truth: the order. But what if you could influence that order before it's even placed—gently guiding the customer toward a choice that aligns better with what your kitchen—or factory—is ready to deliver? That, dear reader, is the art of demand shaping. And much like suggesting the chef's special to a curious diner, it's all about steering demand without sacrificing delight.

In a restaurant, demand shaping is second nature. The kitchen is running low on duck confit, so the waitstaff subtly promotes the short rib special. The pastry chef is short on raspberries, so the server raves about the chocolate tart. In supply chain terms, we call this "influencing the demand curve"—nudging customers toward configurations, lead times, or volumes that align better with supply realities.

For the semiconductor world, this might mean recommending an alternate build spec with faster material availability, bundling configurations to level loading across production lines, or even offering incentives for volume flexibility. A fabless chipmaker in Korea, for example, worked with top-tier OEM customers to shift their demand from constrained 300mm wafers to 200mm alternatives with available capacity. By pairing this with a slight pricing discount and advance delivery promises, the company eased pressure on their foundry slots and improved fulfillment rates across the board.

Smart demand shaping isn't about saying "no" to customers—it's about saying "what if?" It's a conversation, a collaboration. Sales, marketing, and operations must coordinate like a front-of-house and back-of-house dream team. Clear communication channels, regular forecast check-ins, and robust scenario planning tools enable commercial teams to proactively steer demand in ways that serve both the customer's needs and the company's capabilities.

Let's not overlook the power of configurability. When Apple streamlined iPhone options years ago, they didn't just simplify the customer experience—they reduced the number of SKUs, smoothed production sequencing, and gave suppliers fewer flavors to juggle. Similarly, in semiconductor supply chains, rationalizing the "menu" of part numbers and packaging variants can tame the chaos and free up precious capacity. Customers don't always need twelve seasoning options; they want reliability, speed, and quality.

Another potent tool in the demand-shaping arsenal is lead time negotiation. If a customer requests immediate delivery of a low-volume, high-mix part, supply chain teams can offer a trade: an extended lead time for a better price or a volume commitment for expedited service. It's the supply chain version of, "We can get that for you—but would you be open to an off-menu pairing?"

Technology plays a role, too. AI-based demand sensing tools can identify early patterns in customer behavior—allowing commercial teams to preemptively shape the mix. It's like noticing that everyone is asking about vegan options before they even walk in the door—and prepping accordingly.

In the end, demand shaping is not manipulation—it's strategic menu design. It's knowing what's in your pantry, what's about to expire, and what you can whip up quickly and brilliantly. Done right, it delights customers, eases operational stress, and turns reactive firefighting into proactive orchestration.

Buffering and Flexibility - Preparing for the Unexpected Without Overcooking

Even in the most precise kitchens, things go sideways. A delivery of scallops arrives late. A sous-chef calls in sick. A VIP guest demands a five-course vegan tasting menu during steak night. That's why every great chef builds in a buffer—a little wiggle room to handle the chaos. In the world of supply chain, this buffer comes in many forms: safety stock, flexible labor, alternative suppliers, and capacity reserves. But the trick isn't just having a buffer—it's knowing how much, where, and when to use it without burning the budget.

Let's start with the concept of inventory buffers. These are your emergency rations—the extra components or raw materials you keep on hand in case demand surges or supply falters. But stocking too much? That's like prepping 50 soufflés for a dinner party of 12. It clogs the freezer, ties up your cash, and leads to spoilage—or, in semiconductor terms, obsolescence. One leading OSAT in Malaysia tackled this by implementing dynamic safety stock levels tied to customer consumption data and forecast volatility. The result? A 28% reduction in excess inventory and better responsiveness to late-stage demand changes.

Next is capacity buffering. This is your backup oven or extra workstation, ready to fire up when volume spikes. In chip assembly, it may take the form of flex lines or shared-tool capacity across different modules. At a packaging site in Penang, planners created a "swing line" that could pivot between two product families based on real-time demand signals. When one product surged, the line flipped seamlessly —like moving from brunch to dinner service with no lost motion.

Then there's the underrated hero: labor flexibility. Cross-trained staff who can move between inspection, assembly, and packing provide agility that no software can replicate. Think of it like a line cook who can do pastry in a pinch. One U.S.-based wafer fab instituted a rotation program that trained operators across three tools. During an unexpected tool-down event, the site avoided line stoppage by redeploying staff—preserving throughput and morale alike.

Supplier flexibility is another flavor worth exploring. Multi-sourcing, dual-site qualification, and vendor-managed inventory (VMI) all create shock absorbers in your supply chain. When a key substrate supplier in Japan faced a power outage, a U.S. customer switched production to a second qualified source in Taiwan with minimal disruption—thanks to a playbook developed during earlier S&OP reviews.

And what about digital flexibility? Control towers, simulation models, and what-if planning engines are like the kitchen's smart thermostat—adjusting conditions in real time. A global IDM used SAP IBP (Integrated Business Planning) to simulate supply chain stress scenarios and found it could reduce buffer inventory by 15% just by rebalancing site-level production priorities.

The golden rule of buffering: don't hoard; strategize. Buffers should be intentional, monitored, and continuously adjusted. Too little, and you're undercooked. Too much, and you're bloated. The sweet spot? Just enough to catch the chaos—without compromising flavor, flow, or financial discipline.

So, as you prepare your supply chain mise en place, remember: flexibility is the new agility. Up next, we'll stir the pot even more by diving into the role of visibility and communication—because even the best timing and buffers fail if no one hears the dinner bell ring.

Bon appétit!

5

MANAGING KITCHEN CHAOS - RISK MITIGATION STRATEGIES

Understanding Risk in the Supply Chain

IN THE CULINARY WORLD, disaster rarely announces itself—it simply arrives, uninvited and unwelcome, like a soufflé collapsing right as the critic takes their seat. In the global supply chain kitchen, risk behaves the same way. It doesn't always scream fire; sometimes it simmers until the pot boils over. Understanding risk isn't just an academic exercise—it's essential mise en place. It's what separates seasoned chefs from short-order cooks, and resilient supply chains from those that crumble at the first tremor.

In semiconductor operations, where margins are razor-thin and product cycles tight, the stakes are even higher. A single missed delivery, a sudden shift in government policy, or an unseen cyber vulnerability can ripple through the entire ecosystem. As a global commodity manager, you don't just watch for risk—you sniff for it like a chef inspecting the morning catch. It's not about fearing disruption; it's about anticipating it, prepping for it, and being ready to stir the pot before it scorches.

Take, for example, the abrupt factory shutdowns in China during the COVID-19 outbreak. Entire production lines halted overnight—not due to a lack of demand, but because no one had built in time to source alternative suppliers or plan for prolonged lockdowns. Those with foresight—who had done their mise en place far better.

Just like in a kitchen, risk awareness isn't one person's job—it's embedded in the culture. It's in the way procurement checks for geopolitical dependencies, how planners forecast with buffers for the unexpected, and how engineering collaborates to design flexibility into the build. And yes, sometimes it's in the way you choose to react when the sauce separates—do you toss the dish or whip up a quick save?

Whether it's hurricanes disrupting ocean freight lanes, labor strikes slowing port operations, or material shortages from geopolitical flare-ups, risk is part of the recipe. But with the right mindset and preparation, it doesn't have to ruin the service. It becomes part of the rhythm—a challenge that sharpens your edge, keeps your team agile, and inspires creative workarounds that sometimes lead to innovation.

In this chapter, we'll slice into the layers of risk: identifying hidden disruptions, mapping your supply chain's weak spots, exploring resilient sourcing strategies, and contingency planning that's actually executable, as well as the game-changing role of technology. We'll garnish these lessons with real-life examples—from the kitchen floor to global chip fabs—showing how organizations danced with chaos and still served a five-star performance.

So sharpen your knives, fire up your risk radar, and let's get to it. Because in supply chain, like in any great kitchen, chaos isn't a threat —it's an ingredient. And managing it well? That's the secret sauce.

Identifying Potential Disruptions

Disruptions in the supply chain aren't always loud. They don't always barge into your kitchen yelling, "Fire!" More often, they sneak in like a slow gas leak—silent, cumulative, and deadly if undetected.

Identifying potential disruptions is less about panic and more about perception. It's about knowing where the cracks might form before the soufflé falls and treating "what if" not as paranoia but as prudent mise en place.

In a professional kitchen, any chef worth their apron knows where failure hides: a dull knife, an unstable sauce, or that overworked oven that flames out mid-service. In the semiconductor supply chain, the same principle applies—except instead of "béchamel," you're handling backend testing wafers, and instead of burnt toast, you're looking at multi-million-dollar line stoppages.

Let's break it down: disruptions can come from anywhere. Internal process failures, external geopolitical shifts, sudden labor strikes, supplier bankruptcies, logistics delays, natural disasters—you name it. One weak link, and the whole menu is off. The 2021 Suez Canal blockage? That wasn't just a shipping mishap—it was a wake-up call that a single ship, stuck sideways, could back up supply chains for weeks across five continents. Like running out of eggs before the brunch rush—except this time, it's substrates and advanced packaging tools.

In semiconductor operations, long lead times and tightly synchronized manufacturing stages make disruption detection all the more critical. If your die attach epoxy supplier in Malaysia misses a beat, it cascades upstream and downstream faster than a flambé gone rogue. That's why identifying potential disruptions must become muscle memory—built into sourcing strategies, forecasting models, and supplier reviews.

Smart organizations bake this awareness into every layer. They use tier mapping to see beyond Tier 1 suppliers—digging deeper into where their suppliers source from and where those suppliers source from. It's like tracing your vanilla bean back to the exact orchid farm in Madagascar. Precision matters.

One fabless chip company used scenario modeling to identify what would happen if just one of their top five substrate suppliers failed.

That insight led to a diversification strategy that reduced exposure by 40% over 18 months. Another major OSAT in the Philippines ran tabletop "black swan drills," practicing responses to hypothetical events like typhoons, cyberattacks, or pandemic-related labor disruptions. When real disruptions came, they didn't scramble—they executed.

The truth is, if you wait to identify disruption when it arrives, you're already too late. The best supply chains don't just reactively cook—they prepare proactively. Because whether you're plating a meal or delivering microchips, the unexpected isn't an excuse; it's an inevitability.

Mapping Vulnerabilities: Finding the Cracks Before They Break

Before you fire up the burners, a seasoned chef does one crucial thing—identifies where the dish could fall apart. Is the fish too delicate for the grill? Will the sauce split if held too long? Are you relying on a single sous-chef to plate for 50 covers? These vulnerabilities, if unaddressed, become the seeds of disaster.

Supply chains operate no differently. Mapping vulnerabilities is about exposing those pressure points before they blow—before one burnt "béarnaise" turns into a full kitchen shutdown.

In the world of semiconductors, where you're managing everything from raw wafer starts to final package testing across multiple geographies and vendors, blind spots are especially dangerous. Your weakest link might not even be visible on your tier-one radar. It could be a sub-supplier in Vietnam making lead frames or a specialty gas vendor in South Korea. And when that link breaks, it's not just one dish that fails—it's the whole dinner service.

Mapping vulnerabilities begins with a comprehensive supply chain risk audit. Think of it as a culinary pre-service checklist, but instead of checking for clean knives and fresh produce, you're checking for geopolitical hotspots, single-source dependencies, overbooked logistics lanes, and outdated IT infrastructure.

Start by asking: "Where are we most exposed? Where do we lack redundancy? Where is our sourcing overly concentrated by region, supplier, or technology? You wouldn't build a menu where every dish hinges on truffle oil from one supplier—why let your fab depend on a single source for ceramic substrates?"

A leading chipmaker once discovered that 60% of its most critical components came from just two coastal Chinese ports. A regional typhoon disrupted both, halting production at two major OSAT partners. Post-crisis, they implemented a logistics reshuffle and began multi-sourcing with inland backup options. A simple mapping exercise saved them millions in future downtime.

Beyond suppliers and logistics, vulnerabilities also exist in internal systems—manual data entry, siloed communication, or outdated planning tools can cause just as much chaos. One fab in Arizona found that late-stage reschedules were happening due to engineering changes not flowing properly to procurement. A digital workflow revamp resolved the issue, preventing material mismatches and urgent expedite charges.

And don't forget the human element. Skills gaps, tribal knowledge, and over-reliance on key personnel can be as risky as any vendor shortfall. Cross-training, documentation, and process audits keep the kitchen humming even if the executive chef takes a day off.

Ultimately, mapping vulnerabilities isn't about fearing the worst—it's about preparing for it. Because in the kitchen or the supply chain, you can't eliminate risk entirely. But when you know where it hides, you can minimize its bite and keep service running—on time, plated hot, and chaos-free.

Resilient Sourcing Strategies: Stocking the Pantry Before the Storm

Imagine you're prepping a lavish seven-course meal for a surprise VIP guest—and just before service, your only crate of imported sea urchin doesn't show up. Panic? Maybe. Or maybe, if you're a master chef, you've got a local supplier on speed dial or a backup menu that still wows. That's resilience in sourcing: not just having a Plan B, but building a kitchen that can pivot without dropping the knife.

In global supply chains, especially in semiconductors where lead times are long and materials are highly specialized, resilient sourcing isn't optional—it's survival. It's the culinary equivalent of keeping alternative ingredients stocked, having multiple prep cooks cross-trained, and knowing which dishes can flex with little compromise on quality.

For many companies, resilience begins with **multi-sourcing**—establishing more than one qualified supplier for critical materials. It sounds obvious, but it's amazing how many supply chains remain dependent on a single vendor for niche components, especially in legacy nodes or rare-earth-dependent processes. One wire bond manufacturer we worked with sourced 90% of a key gold alloy from a single foundry in Malaysia. A regional flood shuttered operations for three weeks, disrupting downstream customers across two continents. Afterward, they onboarded a secondary partner in India, even though the cost was marginally higher, just to avoid being cornered again.

Geographic diversification is another form of culinary insurance. If your entire pantry is in one place, one fire—or one geopolitical hiccup—could leave you scrambling. That's why companies are now looking beyond China to Southeast Asia, India, and Mexico for second sources. Just as a chef wouldn't rely solely on imports for fresh herbs, savvy supply chain pros are blending local and global sourcing to hedge against volatility.

Then there's **supplier collaboration**. Don't just order ingredients—build partnerships. Joint development programs, quarterly business reviews, and early supplier involvement in design phases allow vendors to forecast demand, invest in capacity, and manage their own risk more effectively. One chip packaging company co-invested with a ceramic substrate vendor to scale capacity at a regional hub. When demand spiked unexpectedly, they were the only customer to receive full allocation—because they helped build the oven.

Qualification and onboarding of alternate suppliers must be done before the fire alarm rings. That means aligning specs, testing capabilities, securing regulatory approvals, and setting expectations. Prequalifying a vendor mid-crisis is like interviewing a new sous-chef mid-dinner rush—not ideal and likely to burn something.

Finally, don't overlook **financial resilience**. A resilient supply base is one that's stable—not always the cheapest. It pays to monitor your vendors' financial health. If a key supplier can't weather a cash flow storm, you might feel the shockwave in your own P&L. Scorecards and supplier health dashboards help flag risks early—before they boil over.

Resilient sourcing isn't just a procurement strategy; it's a mindset. It's about thinking like a chef who knows the market, trusts their network, and plans for the unexpected. Because in the end, no one remembers that your lobster supplier fell through—they remember whether you still served something unforgettable.

Contingency Planning That Actually Works: When the Sauce Splits

In every serious kitchen, there's an unspoken rule: plan for the unexpected. The meat might overcook, the burner might sputter, or the delivery guy might forget the truffles. Great chefs don't just roll with it —they've rehearsed every pivot. The same holds true for global supply chains. A robust contingency plan isn't just a binder on a shelf. It's the action plan you can execute with the speed and precision of a kitchen brigade responding to a flaming pan—controlled, swift, and practiced.

Too often, contingency planning in the supply chain sounds great on a slide deck but fails in practice. It's the culinary equivalent of buying a fire extinguisher and storing it behind three locked doors. What we need are plans that are designed for action—real-time playbooks with clear roles, muscle memory, and tools that support fast, decisive moves.

Start with **buffering strategically**. No, we're not talking about hoarding every possible component like you're prepping for a culinary apocalypse. But for high-risk, long-lead items—say, ceramic substrates or ABF laminates—it makes sense to hold minimal safety stock or collaborate with suppliers on vendor-managed inventory. At one semiconductor test site in Malaysia, planners created tiered stocking strategies for critical items tied to revenue exposure. The result? A 40% reduction in production loss during an unexpected logistics delay. The dish didn't burn; the chef just moved to the next station.

Next comes **scenario simulation**—your kitchen dress rehearsal. Use digital twins or basic what-if modeling to walk through plausible disruptions. What if a key supplier goes offline for 30 days? What if ocean freight delays double? Simulating these scenarios is like running through a mock dinner service: it reveals the soft spots, trains the crew, and gives you a playbook when the pressure is on. Teams that rehearse don't panic—they pivot.

Cross-training your workforce is another staple. Think of it as teaching your pastry chef to handle the sauté station in a pinch. When a shipment gets stuck or a tool goes down, having cross-functional coverage ensures production doesn't screech to a halt. One fab in Oregon launched a "contingency crew" initiative—engineers and planners trained in multiple process areas and supplier escalations. It paid off during a supplier site fire when the rapid reallocation of tasks saved millions in potential downtime.

Lastly, **communication protocols** are everything. Your contingency plan should include a rapid-response communication tree: who calls whom, within how many minutes, using what channel. One company built a Slack-based "supply chain war room" during the peak COVID-19 chaos—no email delays, just fast intel, clear decisions, and immediate action.

Contingency planning that actually works is the difference between scrambling mid-service and confidently finishing the dinner rush. It's not about expecting perfection; it's about preparing to recover quickly, with your team, tools, and timing aligned.

The Role of Technology in Risk Management: Digital Sous-Chefs to the Rescue

If chaos is part of the kitchen, then technology is your most trusted sous-chef—always alert, never flustered, and somehow everywhere at once. In the evolving world of supply chain risk management, digital tools don't just make life easier; they make resilience possible. From real-time visibility to predictive analytics, technology equips us with sharper knives, better prep lists, and the foresight of a chef who knows exactly when the soufflé will fall.

In semiconductor supply chains, where timing, precision, and volume are everything, you simply can't "eyeball" risk anymore. It's no longer enough to ask if something might go wrong. You need to know when, where, how severe, and what the backup plan should be. That's where digital risk management platforms step in—replacing whiteboards and spreadsheets with cloud-based dashboards that visualize every ingredient, tool, and hand in motion.

Let's start with **supply chain visibility platforms**. These tools act like the expeditor on the line—monitoring every order, shipment, and status update in real time. If a component is delayed at port, if a vendor's region is hit by a monsoon, or if a production tool goes down unexpectedly, these systems alert your team instantly. Think of it as that sous-chef yelling, "Behind you!" before a collision occurs—preventing mishaps before they snowball into service disasters.

Then there's the magic of **IoT sensors and smart tracking**. When embedded into containers, packages, or even critical semiconductor components, these devices become your eyes and ears in transit. A vendor shipping ABF substrates from Osaka can now provide real-time humidity, shock, and temperature data en route. If the sensor flags a deviation, your system pings the planner instantly—rerouting the load or pulling backup stock before your wafer line feels the impact. That's not just monitoring; that's prevention in action.

But the true game changer is **predictive analytics**. With machine learning algorithms digesting years of operational and market data, supply chains can now forecast risks like a chef predicting the brunch rush based on weather and Yelp traffic. These tools can warn of upstream material shortages, freight capacity squeezes, or even factory utilization risks weeks in advance. One fabless chipmaker saw a 28% drop in expedite costs simply by using predictive alerts to adjust order timing and shipping mode before disruption hit.

Even **simulation technology**—like digital twins—lets you rehearse risk responses. You can test what happens if a key site in Korea shuts down or if output drops due to labor shortages in the Philippines. It's like running a mock dinner service with your crew, seeing where chaos might emerge and adjusting your staffing and prep accordingly.

Lastly, **collaboration tools**—from Slack war rooms to shared cloud platforms—accelerate crisis response. Cross-functional teams can resolve issues live, with shared data and direct vendor input. Gone are the days of ping-ponging emails and version-controlled spreadsheets. In the middle of disruption, speed is everything—and tech makes that speed possible.

Technology doesn't replace people—it empowers them. It turns your planners into conductors, your buyers into early-warning analysts, and your suppliers into synchronized partners. In the face of disruption, these digital sous-chefs don't panic—they prep, pivot, and plate with confidence.

Because in the high-heat kitchen of semiconductor supply chains, it's not about eliminating chaos. It's about having the tools—and the talent —to dance with it and still deliver a dish worth remembering.

Case Studies: Real-World Kitchen Fires

Every chef has a story—the time the oven caught fire five minutes before service, or when 40 lobsters arrived instead of 4. These aren't just war stories; they're hard-earned lessons that shape how kitchens prepare for the next big curveball. In supply chain management, real-world disruptions are the ultimate stress tests, and the scars they leave often rewrite playbooks industry-wide.

Let's begin with **Toyota**, a master of lean but also once a cautionary tale. In 2011, the Tōhoku earthquake and tsunami hit Japan and disrupted thousands of suppliers across the automotive and electronics industries. Toyota's production halted—not just from direct damage, but because many of its suppliers were sole-sourced and located in the affected area. Their takeaway? Visibility beyond tier one. The company responded by building a comprehensive supplier database tracking more than 400,000 parts and their geographic locations. That digital pantry gave them the ability to react quickly, reroute procurement, and redesign continuity plans. It was a hard lesson—but it turned into resilience.

Cisco, another high-stakes player in the semiconductor world, built its reputation not just on networking gear but on its ability to navigate turbulence. Its Supply Chain Risk Management (SCRM) program integrates predictive analytics and real-time alerts to model global disruptions—from trade shifts to supplier distress. In 2020, when COVID-19 froze much of the world's logistics, Cisco was able to rebalance supply allocations in real time, minimizing product delays while competitors scrambled. They didn't just react—they adapted mid-flight.

Then there's **Intel**, which weathered the pandemic storm through a multi-pronged approach. Knowing that COVID-19 would rattle everything from raw materials to skilled labor, Intel didn't wait. They activated a tiered response strategy—ramping up alternate sourcing, reserving critical capacity at OSATs, and chartering dedicated freight when air cargo space became scarce. Intel also leaned heavily on internal scenario planning simulations, allowing it to prioritize which product lines to keep moving based on revenue impact and customer urgency. Like a Michelin-starred kitchen with limited burners, it cooked what mattered most first—and delivered.

Even outside the semiconductor world, **Unilever** offers a savory example. They deploy scenario planning on a global scale—anticipating how political unrest, drought, or economic shifts might affect their ingredient sourcing. Their "climate-adaptive" sourcing models helped them stay ahead during weather-related crop failures, ensuring that their product lines continued to flow while competitors faced shortages and reformulations.

What ties all these companies together isn't luck. It's vigilance, playbook precision, and the courage to learn from disaster. Each "kitchen fire" sharpened their tools and refined their recipes for resilience. They didn't throw out the dish—they innovated, iterated, and served it hotter the next time around.

In every great kitchen, chaos is not the enemy—it's the crucible. The same is true for supply chains. Fires flare up. Ingredients run short. Orders pile in unexpectedly. But the mark of a resilient operation isn't the absence of chaos—it's the ability to work through it with confidence, creativity, and cohesion.

Throughout this chapter, we've explored how to sense disruptions before they simmer, map out fragile points in your process, and prepare with the precision of a chef assembling mise en place for a 12-course tasting menu. We've unpacked how smart sourcing strategies act like pantry backups, how technology can be your digital sous-chef, and how leading companies—from semiconductor giants to consumer brands—have turned uncertainty into opportunity.

Now, as you ladle these lessons into your own operations, remember: managing risk isn't just about reaction—it's about rhythm. It's about building a kitchen where every team member knows their station, every process has a backup, and every contingency is rehearsed like a signature dish. It's about planning so thoroughly that even when the oven breaks or the truffle delivery is late, you can still plate with pride.

In the semiconductor world, where precision and speed are paramount and the margin for error is thinner than a wafer, resilience isn't a luxury—it's the foundation. And just like a chef adapts to a last-minute ingredient swap without breaking stride, a great supply chain adapts to the unexpected with poise.

So embrace the flames. Sharpen your knives, but also your foresight. Make chaos your canvas, and let resilience be the flavor you layer into every decision. Because when your supply chain runs with culinary confidence, even the messiest of moments can serve up a masterpiece.

Bon appétit—and may your risk strategy always be well seasoned.

6

THE POWER OF FLAVOR – INNOVATING WITH TECHNOLOGY

The Secret Sauce: Why Innovation Is the Flavor Every Supply Chain Needs

EVERY CHEF KNOWS that flavor isn't just a finishing touch—it's the soul of the dish. And in supply chain management, especially in the high-stakes semiconductor world, **innovation** is the flavor that transforms a basic operation into a signature experience. Without it, even the most well-organized processes risk becoming bland, outdated, or worse—irrelevant.

Technology is no longer just a garnish on the side of your operational plate—it's the main ingredient. Today's semiconductor ecosystem demands agility, traceability, speed, and precision. From the raw wafer to the finished chip, every step of the process requires a level of sophistication that would make even a Michelin-starred chef sweat. And it's technology that makes it possible.

Imagine trying to run a modern kitchen with only a wood-fired stove and handwritten recipes. That's what relying on legacy systems feels like in today's global supply chain. Gone are the days when spreadsheets and tribal knowledge could carry a team through production peaks or unexpected delays. Modern kitchens—and modern supply chains—thrive on smart tools: ERP systems that sync like kitchen timers, IoT sensors that act like digital taste buds, and AI models that sense the heat of the room like a head chef mid-service—knowing when to fire the mains, hold the garnish, or cool the tempo before something burns.

Let's take predictive analytics, for example. In the kitchen, it's like knowing how many soufflés you'll need before the dinner rush hits. In supply chains, it means forecasting demand swings and adjusting your procurement or logistics accordingly. One leading semiconductor packaging facility in Malaysia adopted AI-driven demand planning, which reduced inventory holding by 18% and improved order fulfillment time by nearly a week. That's the power of flavor—served smart.

Technology also democratizes excellence. Just as "sous-vide" and combi ovens have leveled the playing field in fine dining, digital dashboards and MES platforms empower even small or mid-sized suppliers to meet the same quality and speed expectations as their global counterparts. With visibility tools, quality controls, and agile production sequencing, a once-fragmented operation becomes an orchestrated ballet.

And don't forget the front-of-house experience—because customers feel the flavor, too. Order tracking portals, real-time shipment visibility, and AI-powered customer service chatbots turn what used to be a black box into a transparent experience. It's like giving your guests a behind-the-scenes tour of your kitchen—building trust while serving up excellence.

So, as we begin this chapter, remember: flavor isn't optional. Innovation is what gives your supply chain the edge, the aroma, the character. It's what makes customers come back for more—and what keeps your operation not just afloat but unforgettable.

Let's turn up the heat and explore how the right blend of technology can elevate your supply chain from functional to phenomenal.

Emerging Technologies Stirring Up the Industry

Just as molecular gastronomy reimagined the possibilities of food, today's emerging technologies are transforming the very DNA of supply chains. These aren't your everyday kitchen tools—they're your liquid nitrogen, your blowtorch, your flavor-injecting marvels. In the world of semiconductors and global logistics, they're doing more than adding flair—they're rewriting the recipe book.

Let's start with blockchain, the ultimate truth-teller in your digital kitchen. Think of it like labeling every ingredient jar and documenting every prep step to ensure nothing suspicious slips into the mix. Blockchain delivers immutable records that authenticate parts, verify supplier origins, and ensure quality hasn't been compromised along the journey. For semiconductor supply chains—where counterfeit parts can cause catastrophic failure—this traceability is as essential as knowing which eggs are cage-free and which are past their prime.

Digital twins are another star on the rise. These virtual replicas of your physical supply chain allow you to simulate operations, test disruptions, and tweak processes without any real-world fallout. It's like being able to try five different variations of a soufflé without wasting ingredients. One major OSAT (Outsourced Semiconductor Assembly and Test) player used digital twins to simulate line balancing under various load scenarios. The result? A 12% increase in throughput with no additional headcount—a recipe adjustment that paid off in dividends.

Advanced robotics are no longer a futuristic garnish—they're the high-speed sous-chefs of manufacturing. From AGVs (automated guided vehicles) that navigate warehouse aisles like well-trained runners to robotic arms that place micro-components with sub-millimeter precision, these tools bring both finesse and force to the table. In chip fabs, robotic wafer handling reduces contamination risks, while in back-end packaging plants, robotic tray stackers ensure consistency batch after batch—no "oops, I dropped the plating" here.

Artificial intelligence and machine learning are transforming decision-making. These tools not only process data faster than any human—they learn from it. Imagine an AI engine that forecasts resin shortages based on monsoon patterns or automatically adjusts supplier allocations when a vendor's on-time delivery rate dips below 95%. It's like having a supply chain sommelier who knows your palate better than you do.

Augmented reality (AR) brings collaboration to the next level—especially across geographies. Picture an engineer in Oregon guiding a technician in Penang through an equipment calibration using a live AR overlay. It's the equivalent of having your pastry chef mentor your line cook through a croquembouche—without ever leaving the restaurant.

These emerging technologies are not just bells and whistles. They're reshaping cost structures, improving agility, and helping businesses scale innovation with confidence. But like any high-end kitchen, it's not about cramming every gadget into your drawers. It's about understanding your needs, curating the right tools, and blending them seamlessly into your workflow.

In short, emerging tech isn't just stirring the pot—it's changing what's in it, how it's cooked, and how it's served. And in this new era of culinary creativity meeting semiconductor sophistication, those who embrace the boldest flavors will find themselves setting the next standard.

The Robotic Revolution Is Here

In the modern kitchen of supply chain management, robots are no longer just novelties—they're the seasoned sous-chefs quietly mastering mise en place while the rest of the team scrambles to plate the entrée. The robotic revolution isn't coming; it's already here. And in the high-stakes, high-precision world of semiconductors, it's transforming the very way we prep, plate, and perform.

Let's start with **manufacturing floors**, where robotics have gone from supporting roles to center stage. In semiconductor fabs, automated wafer-handling robots now glide silently between workstations, moving million-dollar materials with micrometer accuracy. No breaks. No fatigue. No contamination. It's like having a line cook who never drops the béarnaise or sneezes into the soufflé. These robotic arms have become essential in managing increasingly complex builds—especially as chip geometries shrink and error margins approach zero.

Over at **OSAT and packaging sites**, robotics take on a different but equally critical role. Tray stackers, component pickers, and automated optical inspection units all work in coordinated harmony—eliminating human variability and increasing throughput. One Southeast Asian chip packaging site integrated robotic pick-and-place arms with AI-driven quality control cameras. The result? A 30% boost in first-pass yield and a reduction in line stoppages that once plagued peak production hours. That's not just efficiency—it's excellence at scale.

Warehousing has also gone gourmet. Smart robots now sort, store, and retrieve inventory with the grace of a maître d' serving a tasting menu. Guided by RFID tags and real-time WMS data, these bots navigate warehouse aisles with uncanny precision. Amazon's Kiva systems may have made headlines, but in the semiconductor world, robotic AGVs are becoming the norm—from ferrying raw materials to replenishing SMT lines without human intervention.

But the real flavor lies in the **integration**. When robotics are synced with IoT sensors, real-time MES dashboards, and predictive analytics, they move from reactive tools to proactive partners. A robotic arm doesn't just pick a component—it knows when to replenish, how to prioritize urgent builds, and when maintenance is due based on usage cycles. It's like a kitchen robot that not only cooks the steak but also orders more ribeye before you run out.

Importantly, this shift doesn't push people out—it **elevates them**. Robotics handle the repetitive, risk-prone tasks, freeing skilled workers to focus on high-value areas like design, quality improvement, and strategic planning. It's the culinary equivalent of moving your best chef off salad duty and into menu innovation. The result? A workforce that's more engaged, more efficient, and more aligned with long-term business goals.

In short, robots aren't replacing the artistry of supply chain—they're enhancing it. Like a precision mandoline in a master chef's hands, robotics bring consistency, speed, and a touch of awe. And when woven into the broader digital fabric, they don't just support the operation—they help redefine what is possible.

Harnessing Data Analytics for Strategic Decision-Making

In any top-tier kitchen, the best chefs don't just cook—they taste, adjust, and refine constantly. They understand the subtle balance of flavors, the timing of each component, and how one small ingredient can make or break the entire dish. In the world of supply chain, data analytics plays that very same role: the quiet force that turns guesswork into gourmet.

Data, when raw, is like unseasoned broth—technically edible but uninspiring. It's only when it's filtered, reduced, and seasoned with insight that it becomes the flavorful foundation for high-performance decision-making. And in semiconductor supply chains, where complexity is layered and speed is critical, that depth of flavor—of intelligence—is everything.

Descriptive analytics tells us what happened—like reviewing a recipe that didn't quite land. Late deliveries, missed production targets, and unexpected downtime get laid bare. This helps supply chain teams learn from past mistakes, identify root causes, and adjust their mise en place going forward.

Then comes **predictive analytics**, the clairvoyant sommelier of the operation. It spots patterns in data and anticipates future outcomes: a spike in lead times during monsoon season, a surge in memory chip demand ahead of a major product launch, or a dip in supplier performance following regional unrest. Predictive models, fed by machine learning, offer advance notice that is as valuable as a sous-chef whispering, "You're going to want to pull that roast early."

And **prescriptive analytics**? That's your executive chef. It doesn't just suggest what might happen—it recommends what to do about it. Should you reallocate stock to a different site? Expedite materials now or wait for the next batch? Should you diversify sourcing or negotiate longer lead times? Prescriptive systems weigh trade-offs, simulate outcomes, and recommend optimized responses faster than a line cook flipping eggs during the brunch rush.

Dashboards have become the "kitchen pass" of the digital world—flashing alerts when a process goes off-temp or inventory levels are low. When powered by AI and connected to real-time data streams, these platforms allow decision-makers to course-correct before a problem becomes a catastrophe. One chip assembly site in Oregon leveraged AI-based analytics to reduce late-order penalties by 40%, simply by identifying recurring demand volatility and adjusting procurement buffers accordingly.

But perhaps the most powerful aspect of data analytics is **continuous refinement**. Just as chefs taste constantly to adjust seasoning, modern supply chain teams must adapt forecasts and planning inputs in real time. Demand signals shift. Customer needs evolve. Supplier dynamics fluctuate. And only those organizations agile enough to recalibrate based on fresh data can maintain their edge.

Ultimately, harnessing data analytics is about turning operational noise into a symphony. It's about creating a system that doesn't just feed you numbers but helps you sense, respond, and lead. When done right, it's not just efficient—it's elegant.

So, keep the data flowing, the insights simmering, and the dashboards sharp. Because in today's supply chain kitchen, the smartest flavor comes from informed intuition—powered by analytics.

Case Study: Apple's Ingredient-First Innovation Strategy

In the world of culinary excellence, some chefs insist on growing their own herbs, sourcing rare spices from far-off lands, or even aging their own cheese—all in pursuit of that perfect flavor. In the tech world,

Apple is that chef. Their approach to supply chain innovation is not merely operational—it's ingredient-first, flavor-forward, and relentlessly refined for perfection.

At the heart of Apple's recipe lies **vertical integration**. Much like a chef who handpicks every tomato, Apple made a bold decision to design its own chips—Apple Silicon. This move pulled the company away from its longtime reliance on Intel and put the creative and logistical reins back in its own hands. It wasn't just about performance; it was about control over the supply chain from seed to plate. By partnering deeply with **TSMC** (Taiwan Semiconductor Manufacturing Company), Apple gained early access to cutting-edge process nodes (5nm and now 3nm), securing not only technological edge but also timing advantage.

This decision rewrote Apple's playbook. It aligned product design, software, hardware, and sourcing like a perfectly calibrated dish. The M1 chip wasn't just fast—it was on time, lean in inventory, and optimized for efficiency. Apple didn't just avoid the global chip shortage—they tap-danced through it while others scrambled for table scraps.

Apple's **ingredient sourcing** doesn't end at silicon. They've elevated **predictive analytics** to an art form, forecasting demand fluctuations with uncanny precision. Their AI-driven demand planning platform is like a Michelin-starred chef tasting the sauce before the guests arrive—it preempts shortages, ensures ideal stock levels, and reduces waste. Their logistics network, customized and integrated globally, allows them to reroute parts like ingredients in a kitchen rush—adjusting recipes without sacrificing the dish.

Then there's automation. Apple's supply chain partners, especially **Foxconn**, deploy tens of thousands of robots to ensure consistency, reduce labor dependency, and safeguard against variability. Like a pastry chef using precision piping tools, these machines ensure every component lands exactly where it should—every time.

What makes Apple exceptional isn't just technology—it's philosophy. They treat the supply chain not as a cost center but as a creative discipline. Every part is curated, every process fine-tuned, and every supplier relationship meticulously managed. Their obsession with quality and timing has transformed what could be a logistical operation into a culinary performance—and they deliver it flawlessly, season after season.

The result? A resilient, vertically integrated supply chain capable of launching global products with nearly flawless execution—even during pandemics and global material shortages. Apple doesn't just source ingredients; it owns the pantry, designs the tools, and writes the menu.

It's not magic—it's mastery. And it's a case study in how the supply chain, when treated as both science and art, becomes the defining ingredient in sustained innovation.

Innovation isn't just about flashy tools or buzzworthy trends—it's about infusing your supply chain with flavor, finesse, and foresight. From AI-driven forecasts to robotic precision, digital twins to real-time dashboards, today's technology isn't just modernizing operations—it's transforming them into agile, intelligent, and high-performing ecosystems. These tools act as your culinary accelerants: enhancing visibility, reducing waste, and cooking up strategies that scale.

Like any great dish, the magic lies in the blend. No single ingredient—whether IoT or analytics—makes the meal. It's the way they're combined, tested, and adapted to your specific operation that creates a competitive edge. Apple, TSMC, Cisco—these aren't just success stories; they're recipes for resilience, served with a side of daring innovation and plated for global impact.

So, whether you're at the pass of a high-tech fab or reviewing inventory in a cloud-based kitchen dashboard, remember: technology isn't here to replace your intuition—it's here to refine it. The chef still runs the kitchen. The tools simply help you plate perfection at scale.

The future of supply chain? It's smart, sensory, and surprisingly flavorful. Bon appétit to that.

Case Study: TSMC - The Silent Architect of Semiconductor Agility

If Apple is the dazzling front-of-house chef plating masterpieces for a global audience, **TSMC**—Taiwan Semiconductor Manufacturing Company—is the masterful sous-chef in the back, orchestrating the high-heat, high-stakes chaos with quiet excellence. You won't often see them center stage, but without TSMC's precision, consistency, and resilience, the dish doesn't get made.

TSMC is the world's largest dedicated semiconductor foundry, and their secret isn't just scale—it's their ability to innovate under pressure while maintaining unflinching quality. They operate like a kitchen running on military timing, where every ingredient arrives just in time, every station hums in unison, and every plate leaves the pass exactly as ordered.

At the heart of their operational brilliance is real-time digital orchestration. TSMC uses digital twins—virtual replicas of their fabs and production networks—to simulate every step of manufacturing before the first silicon is etched. It's like a chef pre-running every recipe in a test kitchen to anticipate burn points, prep times, and plating windows. This allows TSMC to avoid bottlenecks, allocate capacity efficiently, and maintain an uninterrupted flow even amid record-breaking demand.

Their smart factory automation systems are the envy of the semiconductor world. Automated guided vehicles glide between stations, material handling robots work seamlessly in cleanrooms, and IoT-enabled sensors monitor variables like temperature, humidity, and particulate levels—essential in the delicate soufflé-making that is advanced chip production.

But where TSMC really earns its Michelin stars is in strategic risk mitigation. Recognizing the geopolitical fragility of operating solely in Taiwan, TSMC expanded its global footprint with new fabs in Arizona and Japan, baking in geographic redundancy to weather any future disruption. Like any prudent kitchen that sources from multiple farms and regions, TSMC isn't putting all its eggs in one rice basket.

Their collaborative planning with clients, like Apple, Nvidia, and AMD, ensures synchronized demand forecasting and product ramp-ups. These aren't just vendor relationships—they're strategic culinary partnerships, where menu design, ingredient planning, and table timing are all coordinated months in advance.

The impact? TSMC consistently delivers on the tightest timelines in the industry, ramping up next-generation process nodes (like 3nm and soon 2nm) faster than any competitor. Their ability to scale, adapt, and execute through global turmoil—be it the pandemic, supply shortages, or geopolitical tensions—sets a benchmark for what "operational agility" truly means.

TSMC doesn't need to boast. Their results speak for themselves. They are the quiet, confident hand behind the most high-profile tech innovations of our era, ensuring that when the spotlight hits, the dish is hot, perfect, and ready to wow.

Turning Up the Heat: The Final Garnish

Innovation isn't just about flashy tools or buzzworthy trends—it's about infusing your supply chain with flavor, finesse, and foresight. From AI-driven forecasts to robotic precision, digital twins to real-time dashboards, today's technology isn't just modernizing operations—it's transforming them into agile, intelligent, and high-performing ecosystems. These tools act as your culinary accelerants: enhancing visibility, reducing waste, and cooking up strategies that scale.

Like any great dish, the magic lies in the blend. No single ingredient—whether "IoT" or analytics—makes the meal. It's the way they're combined, tested, and adapted to your specific operation that creates a competitive edge. Apple, TSMC, and Cisco—these aren't just success stories; they're recipes for resilience, served with a side of daring innovation and plated for global impact.

So, whether you're at the pass of a high-tech fab or reviewing inventory in a cloud-based kitchen dashboard, remember: technology isn't here to replace your intuition—it's here to refine it. The chef still runs the kitchen. The tools simply help you plate perfection at scale.

The future of supply chain? It's smart, sensory, and surprisingly flavorful. Bon appétit to that.

From Prix Fixe to À La Carte: The Shift Toward Personalization

In the golden age of mass production, the prix fixe menu ruled — standardized offerings, tightly controlled, and engineered for efficiency. Every diner got the same three-course meal, just as every customer got the same product line. It worked in a world that valued predictability over choice. But the future of supply chain is no longer about sameness; it's about personalization. Customers expect their "dish" plated their way, whether it's custom packaging, tailored configurations, or last-minute order changes.

What makes this possible is not just a change in philosophy but a revolution in tools. Technology has become the quiet line cook that makes personalization scalable. AI and machine learning forecast demand variations with uncanny accuracy, helping leaders prepare multiple recipes in advance. Digital twins simulate thousands of "what if" scenarios, ensuring the kitchen isn't caught off guard by sudden requests. Cloud-based CPQ (Configure-Price-Quote) systems let procurement, engineering, and sales collaborate in real time, quoting complex, customized solutions as effortlessly as a maître d' reciting today's specials.

Collaborative platforms take the concept further, letting customers co-design their meal. Instead of dictating from the kitchen, supply chain leaders can invite customers into the recipe process, seeing instantly what's feasible, what it costs, and how long it will take to plate. The result isn't just customization; it's transparency and trust built into every order.

Culinary metaphors abound. A prix fixe menu might have been fast and predictable, but a digitally enabled kitchen can juggle multiple orders — one gluten-free, one extra-spicy, one plated in under ten minutes — without chaos. Technology turns the kitchen into a symphony, synchronizing stations that once worked in silos. In semiconductor terms, this is the leap from rigid product flows to agile, configuration-driven systems where complexity no longer cripples efficiency.

The magic is that personalization, once considered too costly or inefficient, is now repeatable. Technology makes it possible to serve à la carte without losing consistency, to delight without derailing operations. The soufflé rises not just once, but reliably every night of service.

Technology, in short, transforms personalization from a boutique gesture into a scalable recipe. It allows leaders to deliver not only what customers want but also what the business can sustain — efficient, predictable, and deliciously unique.

7

THE CHEF'S SPECIAL - CUSTOMIZATION IN SUPPLY CHAINS

EVERY GREAT CHEF has a signature dish—a creation that speaks to their soul, surprises the palate, and keeps guests coming back. In the world of supply chain, customization is that signature dish. It's where strategy meets creativity, where process yields to personal touch, and where one-size-fits-all becomes one-plate-at-a-time.

Customization is no longer just a competitive advantage—it's the expectation. Whether you're building a bespoke semiconductor for a next-gen device or tailoring packaging solutions for a niche market, customers want something made just for them. And like any great culinary masterpiece, it takes precision, flexibility, and a deep understanding of ingredients to pull it off.

Gone are the days of mass production ruling the kitchen. Now, agility, modularity, and responsiveness are the new mise en place. In this chapter, we'll explore how to craft tailored experiences across your supply chain—from engineering and procurement to final delivery—without compromising quality, cost, or speed.

We'll also dive into flavor-packed examples from chipmakers who blend customization with scale, techniques to avoid the pitfalls of overcomplication, and the secret to keeping your operations nimble while still delivering that "special something."

So grab your tongs, fine-tune your plating, and get ready to design supply chains that not only meet demand but also delight the end customer.

From Prix Fixe to À La Carte: Personalization for the Customer's Plate

Chapter 6 was about the tools in the kitchen; this chapter is about the diner at the table. Because at the end of the day, technology alone doesn't justify personalization — the customer does. The world of supply chain has shifted from efficiency at scale to differentiation at the plate. Just as no two diners walk into a restaurant with identical tastes, no two customers want the same chip, package, or delivery schedule.

In semiconductors, the range of appetites is staggering. One customer demands ultra-low latency, another needs extreme power efficiency. An automotive ECU supplier insists on thermal resilience for desert climates, while a gaming company craves maximum speed with zero lag. Each order is like a diner with precise dietary restrictions — no onions, gluten-free, extra heat — and the kitchen must deliver without delay or compromise.

This customer-centric personalization pushes supply chains to adapt far beyond old production lines. Standardized wafers or modular components may provide a base recipe, but the plating — the final assembly, testing, and delivery — is tailored to each client's taste. Flexible fulfillment, modular design, and postponement strategies act like the garnish station: they allow the chef to add the final flourish that makes the dish feel uniquely prepared, even though the kitchen is running on shared prep.

The risk of getting this wrong is enormous. A customer who feels ignored won't just send the dish back — they'll leave the restaurant. In global supply chains, that means losing market share to competitors who understood the nuances of personalization. Leaders who embrace customization as part of the experience, rather than an inconvenient exception, build loyalty that lasts longer than any single product cycle.

And here lies the leadership lesson. To personalize effectively, one must balance operational efficiency with empathetic service. It's not enough to have the tools — the "digital sous-chefs." You must also cultivate the instinct of the head chef who knows when a diner is about to complain, when to adjust the seasoning, and when to simply serve with confidence.

True personalization is validated not by the system that produces it, but by the customer who savors it. It's a shift from what the kitchen can cook to what the diner truly wants to eat — and that's where enduring competitive advantage lies.

Modular Menus: Designing Flexible Supply Chains for Customization

If customization is the modern diner's demand, then modularity is the chef's answer. In the culinary world, this is akin to preparing mise en place so thoroughly that you can whip up anything from a Thai curry to a vegan risotto without skipping a beat. It's not about having everything—it's about having the right things ready to go in a way that's adaptable, scalable, and fast. In supply chain terms, this is the art and science of modular design.

At its core, modularity means breaking down a product or system into interchangeable, reusable components. Think of it like a tasting menu where core ingredients—say, grilled protein, a starch base, and seasonal veg—can be assembled in countless combinations. For supply chains, modular design allows organizations to meet diverse customer demands without reengineering the wheel every time. Instead of starting from scratch with each custom order, you're remixing well-prepared parts into new, made-to-order offerings.

This strategy is gaining traction in semiconductor and electronics manufacturing, where high-mix, low-volume (HMLV) models are becoming the norm. Products are built using standardized modules—like base dies, substrates, or I/O configurations—that can be quickly tailored to specific applications. Whether it's a high-performance GPU or a power-efficient SoC for wearables, modularity allows suppliers to serve up tailored solutions with speed and consistency.

But modularity isn't just about product architecture—it's a philosophy that must extend across procurement, manufacturing, logistics, and even service. Consider how modular BOMs (Bills of Materials) allow for greater visibility and substitution options in the face of shortages. Or how modular packaging allows for multiple customer branding options using a single base material. The key is building flexibility into every layer of the operation.

To truly master modularity, companies must rethink their kitchen layout—figuratively and literally. This may mean reorganizing factories into flexible work cells, adopting SMED (Single-Minute Exchange of Die) practices to reduce changeover time, or using predictive analytics to determine which modules will be in highest demand next quarter. It's not just what's in the pantry; it's knowing when and how to use it.

And let's not overlook the role of digital infrastructure. PLM (Product Lifecycle Management) systems help manage version control across variants. MES (Manufacturing Execution Systems) enables dynamic scheduling. And supplier collaboration tools ensure that upstream partners are as agile as the production floor.

Ultimately, modular design doesn't just tame the chaos of customization—it makes it profitable. Like a great chef prepping for the unexpected rush, a modular supply chain stays calm, capable, and ready to delight. Because when every customer wants a dish made just for them, it's modularity that keeps the kitchen running and the service smooth.

The Value of Limited Editions: Balancing Efficiency and Exclusivity

In the culinary world, there's something magical about a chef's special—those limited-time offerings crafted from seasonal ingredients or an inspired flash of creativity. It's not just food; it's an experience. And that's exactly what limited-edition products offer in the supply chain world: a taste of exclusivity, a spark of urgency, and a boost to brand identity that mass production simply can't deliver.

But here's the secret: limited editions aren't about throwing efficiency out the window. They're about mastering the delicate balance between customization and operational discipline. Much like a fine dining kitchen that slots in a seasonal tasting menu alongside its staples, savvy supply chains know how to orchestrate small-batch, high-margin products without disrupting core operations.

In the semiconductor and electronics space, limited editions often come in the form of region-specific SKUs, customer-exclusive chip variants, or commemorative packaging. These aren't just vanity plays—they're strategic tools. They help brands test demand, penetrate new markets, strengthen customer loyalty, and even offload surplus materials creatively.

Take the example of a global hardware brand that introduced a limited run of co-branded gaming GPUs featuring custom heatsinks and firmware optimized for niche audiences. By leveraging existing components and modifying only the final assembly and packaging, they created a buzzworthy product with minimal incremental cost. The result? A sellout in days and viral marketing worth millions—all without disrupting their base production.

The key lies in planning. Limited editions need to be scoped with precision: clear MOQs (minimum order quantities), agile supplier alignment, and pre-defined supply chain pathways that prevent bottlenecks. This means collaborating closely with design, marketing, and procurement teams to ensure the right raw materials are available and alternative routing is on standby—like a "pop-up kitchen" prepping for a one-night-only service.

Another trick? Time-boxed production windows. Much like restaurants offering a limited-time seasonal menu, supply chains can streamline resource allocation and create FOMO (fear of missing out) while keeping the factory cadence smooth. Smart use of modular components—such as interchangeable chipsets, socket compatibility, or standardized boards—further reduces overhead while maintaining design freedom.

And don't underestimate storytelling. In a world flooded with choices, narrative sells. Tying limited editions to a product milestone, customer anniversary, or regional celebration adds emotional value that far outweighs the physical cost. It's branding meets logistics—with a dash of culinary showmanship.

So whether it's a tech launch or a specialty SKU, limited editions remind us that supply chains aren't just about throughput and cost—they're about experience and excitement. Like a perfectly plated "amuse-bouche," they delight, surprise, and keep customers coming back for the main course.

Designing for Demand Diversity: Mass Customization without the Mayhem

In the kitchen, chefs dream of crafting each dish to individual taste—less salt here, extra sear there, a vegan twist on a classic coq au vin. But when the dining room fills up and orders are flying, the fantasy of perfect personalization can quickly devolve into pure chaos. The secret? A modular mise en place. Prepped ingredients, smart sequencing, and agile techniques that allow for variation—without burning the kitchen down.

In supply chains, this is the art of mass customization—designing for variety while maintaining the efficiencies of scale. It's the difference between a frantic made-to-order scramble and a graceful, high-volume service with tailored touches. And in today's demand-driven world, it's not a luxury; it's the expectation.

Customers—whether they're ordering a custom PC build or a personalized smartwatch—want to feel like they're getting something made just for them. At the same time, companies can't afford to abandon efficiency or let inventories balloon out of control. So how do we serve up this bespoke experience without sacrificing profitability?

Enter modular design. Think of it like a culinary prep table filled with versatile ingredients that can be recombined in countless ways: a base chipset here, a flexible connector there, customizable firmware over the top. When product architecture is built on swappable modules, suddenly hundreds of SKUs become manageable without a thousand different parts clogging up the line. Dell's "Build Your Own Laptop" model, for instance, doesn't require thousands of unique assemblies—it relies on smart configuration from a standardized base.

The real trick lies in postponement strategies—delaying final configuration until the last possible moment. Much like holding off on dressing a salad until it hits the plate, companies can manufacture generic base units, then customize packaging, software, or final assembly near the customer. This approach slashes lead times, reduces inventory risk, and enables greater responsiveness to real-time demand shifts.

But customization isn't just a product strategy—it's a supply chain culture. It requires collaboration between design, sourcing, planning, and fulfillment. It means engaging suppliers early, investing in flexible tooling, and sharing demand signals further upstream. One semiconductor firm implemented a demand-based build-to-configure model for its analog devices, reducing delivery lead times by 40% while doubling customer satisfaction scores.

Digitization plays a key role here too. AI-powered configuration engines, CPQ (Configure-Price-Quote) tools, and advanced planning systems are like the maître d' who remembers your favorite wine and adjusts the menu just for you—at scale.

Mass customization doesn't mean giving up control. It means building in flexibility by design, empowering teams to adapt without missing a beat. It's like offering the chef's special 50 different ways—while still running a tight kitchen.

The Role of the Customer: Co-Creation, Feedback, and the New Front-of-House

Once upon a time, the customer sat quietly at the table and accepted whatever the kitchen served. No substitutions. No tweaks. Today? The customer walks straight into the kitchen, grabs a spatula, and says, "Let's cook something together."

Welcome to the era of **co-creation**—where customers aren't just end users; they're collaborators in product design, sourcing preferences, and even delivery timing. In the same way a sommelier curates the perfect pairing based on your tastes, modern supply chains are learning to listen, adapt, and even evolve in real time based on customer input.

In semiconductor and electronics supply chains, this shift is especially critical. Custom ASICs, configurable logic, application-specific software layers—none of these come from guessing. They emerge through iterative dialogue between customer and supplier. Think of it as a culinary tasting menu developed on the fly, with the diner giving notes after every course.

This co-creation extends far beyond product features. Customers are weighing in on **sustainability, sourcing ethics, pricing transparency**, and **supply resilience**. They're asking: "Where was this made? Who made it? Can I have it with less carbon, please?" Supply chains are no longer backstage operations—they're part of the brand's story. And the best brands are bringing their customers right into the conversation.

Take Tesla, for example. The company's direct-to-consumer model enables real-time configuration of vehicle features—color, autopilot, battery type—through a simple online portal. But more importantly, Tesla captures data from every driver and uses it to inform hardware tweaks, software updates, and supply chain planning. The car you drive today may actually help shape the car they build tomorrow.

Semiconductor companies are embracing similar approaches. A fabless chip startup, for instance, might launch a developer platform allowing customers to test early-stage silicon designs, submit feedback, and influence the final product architecture. This iterative loop doesn't just drive innovation; it builds loyalty.

And let's not forget the power of **feedback loops**. From NPS surveys to app reviews to in-field sensor data, smart companies ingest customer sentiment like a chef tasting every sauce before service. They don't wait for reviews—they course-correct in real time.

Digital tools make this feedback-action loop seamless. CRM systems, sentiment analysis engines, and collaborative product lifecycle management (PLM) tools act as digital maître d's—translating raw input into strategic adjustments. And just like a great waiter who remembers your last meal, these tools create continuity and trust over time.

The result? A front-of-house experience that's fluid, personal, and delightfully responsive. Because when the customer helps craft the meal, they're far more likely to savor every bite.

Flexible Fulfillment: Serving Up Personalization at Scale

In the golden age of personalization, customers expect more than just the option to "have it their way"—they want it now, their way, and without compromise. For supply chains, this is like running a five-star restaurant where every diner wants a different off-menu dish, cooked to their exact taste, all at once—and still expects it hot and plated to perfection.

This is where **flexible fulfillment** becomes the headliner. It's the culinary equivalent of a kitchen that can switch between soufflés and stir-fry without missing a beat. And in the semiconductor world, it's the art of delivering complex, highly customized products—down to lot-level specs or configuration-specific builds—without sacrificing cost, quality, or delivery speed.

Traditional fulfillment models relied on volume efficiency and forecast predictability. But when you're serving personalized orders in real time, agility becomes king. The question isn't "How much can we make?"—it's "How quickly can we shift gears?"

Enter **modular production strategies**. Much like mise en place stations in a kitchen, modularity allows for reconfigurable production lines and late-stage customization. For example, a substrate vendor might run a standardized base layer but complete the final routing based on last-minute chip design updates. This kind of responsiveness transforms lead time from a liability into a competitive advantage.

Then there's the magic of **postponement**—delaying final product configuration until the latest possible moment in the supply chain. Think of it like prepping a dozen pasta sauces in advance but waiting to toss in the customer's choice of protein until the dish hits the sauté pan. In semiconductor logistics, this might look like shipping blank PCBAs to regional hubs and flashing firmware just before final assembly, allowing for regional or customer-specific SKUs.

Of course, this flexibility hinges on **real-time visibility** and **cross-functional orchestration**. If the supply chain is the kitchen, then systems like ERP, MES, and advanced planning software are the expo line—ensuring orders are sequenced, synchronized, and plated with speed. Integrated data streams allow planners to see changes in demand, shift capacity, reroute inventory, and dynamically allocate labor, all before the dish starts burning.

Amazon has perfected this at a retail scale, using predictive algorithms to stage inventory closer to likely delivery points before the order is even placed. Semiconductor leaders are adopting similar techniques—using AI to predict customer reorders, simulate manufacturing scenarios, and adapt fulfillment strategies on the fly.

In the end, flexible fulfillment is what separates good supply chains from gourmet ones. It's the ability to turn complexity into consistency and turn à la carte expectations into repeat business. Because in today's market, the best supply chains don't just deliver—they serve.

Mass Customization: Scaling the Unique Dish

Once upon a time, supply chains were designed like buffet lines—standardized, efficient, and built for volume. But today's customers don't want what everyone else is having—they want something made just for them, and they want it now. So how do you scale bespoke experiences without blowing your kitchen budget or throwing off your cadence? Enter mass customization—the art of combining personalization with production efficiency. It's like preparing a tasting menu where each dish has a twist, yet the kitchen still runs on clockwork.

In essence, mass customization is about offering tailored solutions without surrendering the advantages of mass production. Instead of crafting each unit entirely from scratch (which would be both costly and time-consuming), smart supply chains build flexibility into core processes, allowing last-minute personalization through modular design, digital workflows, and agile manufacturing.

Think about how you might prep ingredients for a build-your-own pizza bar. You don't make 100 completely different doughs; you make one versatile base. Toppings, sauces, and spices? Those are layered on per customer preference. In semiconductor terms, this could mean producing a common die and then adding differentiated features—such as packaging format, final testing specs, or firmware—based on the specific needs of each customer or region.

The secret sauce? **Configuration-driven systems**. These enable everything from dynamic BOM (Bill of Materials) management to rule-based order processing. With smart configurators, companies can support thousands of product permutations while still maintaining operational control. A major EMS (electronics manufacturing services) provider, for instance, uses AI to predict which configuration options are likely to spike during peak periods and stage component inventory accordingly. This tightens planning, shortens cycle times, and prevents that dreaded "86'd" scenario when a key part goes missing mid-service.

Another ingredient in the recipe is **digitally enabled product lifecycle management (PLM)**. By embedding customization logic early in design—using modular blueprints and digital twins—engineering and supply chain teams can collaborate more seamlessly. A fabless chip company might co-develop a baseboard with multiple socket options, allowing the final assembly site to plug in different modules depending on end-customer specs. This keeps the assembly line moving while giving each customer their own special garnish.

And let's not overlook **additive manufacturing (3D printing)**. For low-volume, high-mix environments or prototype batches, this technology eliminates tooling lead times and supports on-demand builds of unique components—like being able to whip up a one-off garnish without disrupting the rest of the service.

Ultimately, mass customization transforms complexity into a strategic asset. When done right, it delights customers, strengthens brand loyalty, and builds resilience. Because in the kitchen of modern manufacturing, the ability to make every dish feel personal—without burning the rest of the service—is what makes you a culinary innovator.

Collaborative Design: Co-Creation with Customers

In the traditional kitchen hierarchy, the chef dictated the menu, and the diners simply chose from it. But in today's hyper-connected, customer-centric world, diners want a seat at the prep table. They want input, influence, and ideally, a hand in designing the dish itself. Welcome to the era of **collaborative design**, where customers don't just consume—they co-create.

In supply chain terms, this shift is monumental. No longer is product development a closed-door affair driven by internal teams and static roadmaps. Instead, companies are inviting customers—OEMs, strategic partners, even end users—into the design process early and often. It's not unlike asking a regular guest what they would like to see on next week's specials and then building your mise en place around that feedback.

This collaboration isn't just about goodwill—it's about **precision alignment**. When a customer helps shape the specifications of a component or system, you reduce guesswork, eliminate rework, and deliver more targeted solutions. In the semiconductor world, this shows up in joint design efforts for system-in-package (SiP) modules or custom ASICs. Rather than pushing out a standard product and hoping it sticks, fabless companies work side by side with customers to define electrical, thermal, and form factor constraints—sometimes even sharing cleanroom time or simulation tools. The result? Chips that fit like a glove and go from tape-out to volume production faster than ever.

A classic example: a networking hardware giant partners with a leading foundry to design a low-power chip optimized for their next-gen routers. Instead of buying off-the-shelf silicon, they collaborate on every detail—from mask layer optimization to pinout design—ensuring the chip meets thermal targets, footprint constraints, and data throughput needs. This approach shortens integration time downstream, minimizes post-production surprises, and strengthens the long-term vendor relationship.

Tools like **collaborative PLM platforms** and **secure cloud-based design environments** make this possible at scale. Customers can drop comments on schematics in real time, engineers can iterate faster with direct feedback, and procurement teams get earlier visibility into material requirements. It's like running a test kitchen where every guest becomes a sous-chef—refining the recipe before it ever hits the pass.

But this level of collaboration requires a foundation of **trust, transparency, and agility**. Clear IP agreements, fast feedback loops, and cross-functional integration are all vital ingredients. You can't co-create with someone who is left waiting for a response or worrying about data leaks.

When done right, collaborative design doesn't just result in better products—it fosters loyalty, reduces development risk, and makes the supply chain more adaptive to market shifts. It's a reminder that sometimes, the best recipes are written together.

Modular Design and Flexible Manufacturing: Building the Bento Box Supply Chain

Imagine a bento box: neatly arranged compartments, each filled with a distinct yet harmonious dish, customizable depending on taste, dietary needs, or the occasion. Now apply that idea to supply chain design. This is the spirit behind **modular design and flexible manufacturing** —a philosophy that emphasizes configurability, interchangeability, and responsiveness.

In the past, product architecture was monolithic. Change one feature, and you'd disrupt the whole system—like trying to swap the protein in a stew after it has been simmering for six hours. But modular design breaks complex products into discrete, standardized units—modules—that can be individually developed, tested, and swapped without rebuilding the entire recipe. It's like prepping components of a dish separately so you can assemble them à la minute based on each diner's preference.

In the semiconductor industry, this approach shines in areas like mobile devices and automotive electronics. A chipmaker might design a core logic module, a connectivity module, and a power management module—each with defined interfaces. Customers can then mix and match these components to tailor functionality for different products, price points, or markets. The result is a faster time to market, reduced engineering costs, and the ability to pivot without starting from scratch.

On the factory floor, **flexible manufacturing systems (FMS)** bring this modularity to life. Equipment is configured to handle multiple SKUs, small-batch runs, and rapid changeovers—like a kitchen line that can move from sushi to stir-fry to soufflé without missing a beat. Automated tooling, programmable logic controllers, and smart MES

(Manufacturing Execution Systems) ensure that shifting demand signals can be met with minimal downtime.

One high-mix semiconductor packaging plant in Southeast Asia implemented a "recipe card" system for its assembly tools—digitized parameter sets that automatically reconfigure machines for different product families. This cut changeover time by 60% and enabled the team to run smaller, more frequent production lots, reducing inventory risk and increasing customer satisfaction.

Modular design also supports **sustainability goals**. Instead of scrapping an entire board for a failed component, you can isolate and replace just the faulty module—reducing e-waste and enabling circular economy practices. This echoes the culinary wisdom of using every part of the ingredient, minimizing waste and maximizing value.

At its core, modularity is about **empowering choice and scaling complexity** without sacrificing control. Like a bento box that adapts to each eater, a modular, flexible supply chain can respond to evolving customer demands with speed, elegance, and minimal disruption.

The Role of Data in Tailoring the Experience

If modular design is the kitchen layout that enables customization, then data is the maître d' who knows each diner's preferences by heart —no notepad required. In the age of personalization, data isn't just helpful; it's the critical ingredient that turns mass production into made-to-order precision.

Customization starts with knowing what your customer truly wants, and that's where data shines. Consumer insights, market analytics, usage behavior, product feedback loops—all of it feeds into a dynamic pantry of intelligence that lets supply chains prepare for demand not just broadly, but specifically. It's like knowing that a diner likes their steak medium-rare but also prefers it plated with asparagus instead of fries. The more you know, the better you can serve.

In the semiconductor world, this manifests through everything from forecasted product configurations to real-time consumption data across verticals. For example, OEMs in automotive or mobile tech share detailed build plans and usage trends with chip suppliers. In return, those suppliers adjust wafer starts, packaging formats, and testing protocols—not for the "average" order, but for a uniquely informed one. That's data-informed plating at scale.

Take **mass customization** platforms used in the cloud or edge computing sectors. They use customer-driven input—like preferred latency, compute power, or energy profiles—to configure chipsets and subsystems tailored to use cases. And it's not just about design: real-time analytics can adjust sourcing, manufacturing, and delivery windows to match exact needs. Think of it like a kitchen that changes its prep list on the fly based on how many guests want the gluten-free entrée tonight.

Advanced analytics and AI now go a step further: they anticipate preferences before the customer even asks. Machine learning models digest patterns from previous orders, regional preferences, environmental data, and usage stats to suggest optimal product mixes, SKUs, or delivery schedules. It's like a chef who knows you're likely to crave ramen on a rainy day—and starts the broth hours before you walk in.

But this level of personalization also requires **trust and data governance**. You can't tailor what you don't measure accurately—or what you don't have permission to use. Transparent data practices, secure integrations with partners, and standardized data formats ensure that insights are not only actionable but ethical. Without them, you're seasoning blind.

In short, data isn't just a byproduct of operations—it's a driver of relevance. In the kitchen of modern supply chains, it's the ingredient that helps you read the appetite before the order is even placed.

Agile Planning and Demand-Driven Production

In the culinary world, there's a marked difference between preparing for a banquet and cooking for a chef's table. One is about volume; the other is about finesse. Customization in the supply chain demands the latter—and that's where agile planning becomes the star sous-chef. Agile isn't about having more hands in the kitchen; it's about having the right hands at the right time, cooking the right thing.

Traditional supply chains often run on forecast-driven models—think bulk meal prep. You make a hundred portions based on last week's sales and hope demand aligns. But in today's landscape of personalization, that approach can lead to waste, obsolescence, and missed opportunities. Demand-driven production flips the recipe. It's built on responsiveness—adjusting procurement, manufacturing, and fulfillment in near real-time based on actual consumption and shifting needs.

In the semiconductor industry, this shows up in how fabs balance wafer starts with downstream packaging variations. An OEM might require a unique memory configuration for a niche device, but instead of launching a dedicated build line, agile planning allows shared resources to flex around that need. Line setups, test protocols, and packaging flows are re-sequenced dynamically, like a kitchen brigade that shifts from searing steak to slow-cooking short ribs mid-service—without skipping a beat.

What makes this agility possible? It starts with **shorter planning horizons** and more frequent updates. Weekly S&OP (Sales & Operations Planning) cadences evolve into daily or even hourly syncs. Decision-makers aren't buried in quarterly spreadsheets—they're reading the heat of the moment and adjusting the recipe accordingly.

One Asian semiconductor firm revamped its production model to be more responsive to tier-one automotive suppliers. Instead of static quarterly builds, it adopted a rolling two-week demand pulse—integrated into both fab capacity planning and final assembly outsourcing. The result: a 15% increase in on-time delivery and a 20% drop in expedited freight costs. That's not just agility; that's profitability with finesse.

Digitization also plays a starring role here. Cloud-based planning tools, demand-sensing algorithms, and digital twins help simulate and optimize changes before they hit the floor. It's like a test kitchen where you can tweak the sauce before committing to the whole pot.

Ultimately, demand-driven agility is about creating a supply chain that doesn't just **react**, but **adapts**—like a top chef reading the dining room and adjusting the menu in real time. It's the magic that transforms a rigid recipe into an elevated, bespoke experience.

Flexible Manufacturing: Cooking in Small Batches

Think of the difference between a buffet and a tasting menu. Buffets focus on mass production—predictable, standardized, and efficient. But a tasting menu? That's crafted in small, deliberate batches, each plate tailored with care. In supply chain terms, that's **flexible manufacturing**—the heart of modern customization.

In the age of mass personalization, "one-size-fits-all" no longer satisfies the appetite. Customers want options: custom features, limited editions, and region-specific variants. To deliver this, manufacturers must move from bulk production to a more nimble, responsive approach—cooking in smaller, smarter batches.

Flexible manufacturing isn't just about producing less; it's about **reconfiguring quickly**. In the semiconductor world, this might mean switching from one chip package type to another with minimal downtime. It could involve adapting to a custom die stack or pivoting to meet a surge in edge-device demand with an alternative substrate. Just like a kitchen crew that seamlessly moves from plating duck confit to prepping vegan risotto, factories must embrace equipment setups, process flows, and labor shifts that cater to change without chaos.

One OSAT provider in Southeast Asia implemented modular work cells and SMED (Single-Minute Exchange of Die) techniques across its back-end assembly. Instead of treating changeovers as a production burden, they transformed them into a competitive advantage—cutting setup time by over 50% and enabling twice as many SKU variants per week. It was the equivalent of a fine-dining kitchen rolling out new seasonal dishes mid-service—without missing a single order.

But the secret ingredient here is **visibility**. You can't pivot quickly without knowing what's coming. That's where connected systems, IoT-enabled tools, and predictive scheduling step in. Operators receive real-time updates, machines are pre-programmed for swift changeovers, and material availability is checked before a switch is even suggested. It's not chaos—it's choreography.

Flexible manufacturing also empowers sustainability. Smaller batches mean reduced inventory waste, fewer obsolete products, and more efficient resource use. Like chefs sourcing only what they'll use that night, supply chain teams trim excess while keeping freshness—and relevance—at the forefront.

And let's not forget the people side. Cross-trained teams, empowered line leads, and a culture of continuous improvement all fuel the ability to flex. One fab dubbed its model "Just-in-Dish"—a playful nod to "Just-in-Time"—where lines adapt based on daily recipe cards generated by integrated planning tools. The result? Lower cost per unit, higher customer satisfaction, and a workforce that thrived on challenge, not routine.

In a world that craves individuality, flexible manufacturing ensures every order is plated with purpose—and every customer feels like a "guest of honor."

Collaborative Customization: Co-Creating with Customers

In a traditional restaurant, the chef designs the menu, and the diners choose from what's available. But in today's supply chain kitchen, the trend has shifted toward something more intimate—**co-creation**. Think of it as the open kitchen experience where customers aren't just spectators; they're collaborators, helping to shape the final dish.

This is the essence of **collaborative customization**. Rather than serving up static offerings, supply chains now invite customers into the design process, blending their preferences, use cases, and feedback into everything from product features to packaging. It's no longer just about satisfying demand—it's about partnering with it.

In the semiconductor space, this plays out in everything from **chip** design collaborations to custom packaging formats tailored to a specific OEM's thermal and space constraints. Major players like AMD and NVIDIA co-develop architectures with hyperscale cloud providers, ensuring that the final product delivers exactly what the end customer needs—right down to power efficiency, latency response, and modularity. It's like creating a dish for someone with dietary preferences, flavor notes, and a favorite childhood memory—all baked into one perfect bite.

But this kind of customization isn't done on a whim. It requires deep integration across engineering, procurement, and operations. Customer success teams work alongside R&D, while supply chain managers ensure the required parts, partners, and lead times are in place. One leading substrate supplier developed a digital configuration platform that lets customers co-design interposers online, validating thermal specs and stack heights in real time. The result? Design cycles were reduced by weeks, and satisfaction ratings spiked like a soufflé in a hot oven.

The beauty of collaborative customization is also in its feedback loop. Customers become more invested when they help shape the product. They provide richer, more actionable data. And that data—usage patterns, service logs, reorder behavior—becomes the mise en place for future innovation. It's iterative, dynamic, and relational.

There's a cultural element too. Co-creation isn't just a tactic—it's a mindset. It demands transparency, curiosity, and a willingness to listen. Just like a chef who steps out of the kitchen to ask how the meal was, supply chain leaders must engage, ask, and adapt. When you build with the customer, not just for them, you serve up not just a product—but loyalty.

So raise the curtain, invite the diner into the kitchen, and start cooking together. Because in the world of collaborative customization, the best recipes are the ones we write as a team.

Mass Customization: Scaling the Signature Dish

The phrase "mass customization" might sound like an oxymoron—after all, how do you make something both personal and scalable? But this is where the real culinary magic of supply chains comes in. It's like preparing a signature dish for thousands of guests without compromising flavor, flair, or finesse.

In the kitchen, this would be the equivalent of a high-volume restaurant that still hand-sears every steak and whips each sauce to order. In supply chain terms, it's about using flexible processes, smart systems, and modular design to deliver individualized products on a mass scale.

Consider Dell, one of the earliest adopters of this strategy. Their "build-to-order" model allowed customers to choose memory, storage, and screen size—and receive a laptop tailored to their preferences, shipped within days. Behind the scenes, Dell's supply chain was a masterclass in synchronized flexibility: component suppliers were tightly integrated, inventory was kept lean, and final assembly was agile enough to respond to daily demand shifts. It wasn't chaos—it was choreography.

In semiconductors, mass customization might take the form of programmable devices, modular packaging, or die-stacking architectures that let different combinations of performance, power, and size requirements be met from the same base platform. Take Xilinx (now part of AMD), whose FPGA (field-programmable gate array) products allow OEMs to customize functionality after manufacturing. It's like sending a dish partially prepped and letting the diner add their own finishing touches—wasabi or Sriracha, their call.

To make this work, manufacturers lean on modularity and standardization at the sub-component level. Think of it as mise en place on an industrial scale—prepared parts, materials, and assemblies ready to be configured like a modular tasting menu. Flexible tooling, configurable automation, and software-defined production lines become essential ingredients in this model.

Technology is also a key enabler. Advanced planning systems, digital twins, and AI-driven demand forecasting allow companies to simulate different demand scenarios and fine-tune their operations before the first part even ships. These tools are the culinary R&D labs of the supply chain world—perfecting recipes at scale.

Mass customization isn't about compromising; it's about elevating. It gives customers the joy of choice while preserving the efficiencies of scale. When done right, it delivers the best of both worlds: personalization with precision.

Supply Chain Segmentation: Serving Multiple Menus at Once

Imagine walking into a restaurant that offers a tasting menu, à la carte options, a vegan prix fixe, and a kid's menu—all prepared in the same kitchen, by the same team, with no delays or drop in quality. That's not culinary chaos—it's mastery. And in supply chain management, the equivalent is **supply chain segmentation**: building and operating differentiated supply chains within the same enterprise to meet the unique needs of different customer segments, product types, or market conditions.

It's not about one-size-fits-all. It's about tailoring operations to deliver the right level of service, cost, and responsiveness depending on what's being served and who's ordering it.

Let's take a semiconductor example: a fab might serve three types of customers—high-volume smartphone makers demanding rock-bottom cost per wafer, automotive clients requiring zero-defect quality and long-term traceability, and fast-paced AI startups pushing for cutting-edge performance and rapid development cycles. If you try to serve them all using the same kitchen line, someone's order is bound to come out cold—or not at all.

Supply chain segmentation is the strategic decision to separate these service streams. This can happen physically (separate facilities), operationally (different processes or planning systems), or virtually (differentiated planning logic and KPIs within a shared platform).

The result? Greater agility, more relevant service levels, and far less waste.

For example, Cisco famously segmented its supply chain into four flows: innovation, volume, replenishment, and agile. Each was optimized for a different product and customer profile—ensuring that new product introductions weren't bogged down by volume efficiency metrics and that mature products weren't over-engineered with agility features they didn't need. It's like setting up separate prep stations for sushi, pizza, and desserts, each with the right ingredients, tools, and timing.

In real-world kitchens and fabs alike, segmentation requires clarity, discipline, and coordination. It means knowing your customer segments deeply—who needs fast versus flawless, who values cost over customization—and aligning your sourcing, planning, and delivery strategies accordingly.

Modern tools make segmentation scalable: ERP systems can track multiple BOMs and routing options; AI can segment demand patterns dynamically; and dashboards can serve up differentiated metrics across each flow. It's like having smart menus that adjust per guest—and a kitchen that executes each one flawlessly.

Ultimately, segmentation doesn't complicate your supply chain—it clarifies it. It's how you serve multiple "dining rooms" from the same operation without compromising consistency, quality, or delight.

Personalization Through Digital Threads: Stitching Custom Orders into Seamless Execution

In haute cuisine, a personalized dining experience means remembering a guest's favorite wine, dietary restrictions, and even the way they like their steak seared. That kind of memory and seamless service used to belong solely to human intuition. But in the modern supply chain, digital threads are the equivalent of the "maître d's" brain—stitching together data, preferences, and performance in real time across the value chain.

A **digital thread** is more than just connectivity—it's the continuous flow of information that follows a product from concept to consumption. It links design systems, manufacturing lines, quality inspections, logistics providers, and customer feedback loops into a single, dynamic narrative. And when personalization is the goal, it's this thread that ensures your made-to-order soufflé doesn't become a frozen entrée halfway through production.

In semiconductor and high-tech industries, where mass customization is increasingly in demand, digital threads enable configurability without chaos. Think of a chip manufacturer offering custom packaging for each customer's system integration. Without a digital thread tying customer inputs to design specs, production protocols, test criteria, and shipping requirements, the complexity would drown the kitchen. But with a digital thread, each unique order becomes a guided tour rather than a scavenger hunt.

Take Siemens Digital Industries, for example. They've pioneered "digital twin" and digital thread integration across multiple verticals, allowing customers to not only visualize but also simulate and configure highly specialized manufacturing environments. A customer designing a power module can trace its specifications from the initial CAD drawing to real-world assembly instructions—all connected and validated through the digital thread. It's like a guest being able to see their dish prepared from scratch on a holographic screen, with every ingredient and technique documented along the way.

These threads also feed intelligence backward. Product issues in the field trigger alerts upstream—design, sourcing, even supplier selection can be adjusted with near real-time data. In a restaurant, that would be like knowing the truffle oil batch was off before the next dish leaves the kitchen.

Personalization through digital threads requires robust data management, cloud infrastructure, and interoperable systems—but the payoff is immense. It's not just about customization—it's about doing it efficiently, accurately, and at scale. Every custom order becomes part of an orchestrated flow, not an exception.

In the end, digital threads let your supply chain deliver unique dishes at scale—hot, fresh, and exactly how the customer asked for them.

Mass Customization Without the Mayhem

In a perfect world, every guest would have a personal chef—and every customer would have a tailor-made supply chain. But in reality, serving up personalization at scale without burning the kitchen down requires the finesse of a Michelin-starred brigade: organized, agile, and obsessively detail-oriented. That's where **mass customization** enters the scene—a recipe that blends scale and specificity, giving customers what they want without sacrificing efficiency or sanity.

Mass customization isn't about saying "yes" to every whim—it's about designing intelligent variety into your operations. Imagine a bakery that offers dozens of cupcake combinations but uses the same base batter, frosting stations, and packaging flow. That's how semiconductor and electronics companies handle configurable products: standard building blocks assembled in thousands of permutations, often with regional or customer-specific tweaks.

Consider Dell, a pioneer in this space. Their configure-to-order (CTO) model allows customers to choose processors, memory, storage, and graphics cards tailored to their needs. But behind the scenes, this isn't chaos—it's a controlled, rules-based system that maps inputs to optimized workflows, synchronized inventory, and regional assembly lines. Dell doesn't reinvent the oven for every cake; they just fine-tune the toppings before sending it to the pass.

The key ingredient? **"Postponement strategy."** By delaying final product differentiation to the last responsible moment, manufacturers keep upstream processes standardized and cost-effective. A chip fab, for instance, may produce blank die en masse, then customize packaging and testing protocols based on late-stage customer signals. This avoids overcommitting to volatile forecasts while still serving individual appetites.

Technologically, **product lifecycle management (PLM)** tools, **configure-price-quote (CPQ)** engines, and **AI-powered planning systems** are the sous-chefs of mass customization. They ensure that customization rules are enforced, sourcing is aligned, and bottlenecks are anticipated—not discovered mid-shift. Some companies even use machine learning to identify the most common configurations and pre-build those variants to shave lead times.

And don't forget **smart manufacturing platforms**—MES systems that adjust production lines on the fly based on customer specs. Think of it like a pasta station wired into the dining room's brain. The moment table six taps in a gluten-free preference, the station auto-switches to rice pasta—no delays, no chef intervention, just perfectly personalized plating through real-time data.

Mass customization done right offers a winning balance: customers feel heard, operations stay lean, and profitability doesn't melt like a forgotten soufflé. It's not easy, but with the right recipe of modularity, digital support, and agile execution, it becomes repeatable—and scalable.

Co-Creation with Customers: Sharing the Kitchen Pass

In most kitchens, the pass is sacred ground—the place where the chef adds the finishing touch before sending the dish to the guest. But what if, instead of waiting at the table, the guest were invited to lean over the pass and suggest a final sprinkle of herbs or a tweak in plating? Welcome to co-creation—where customers don't just order from the menu; they help write it.

Co-creation flips the traditional supplier-customer relationship on its head. It's no longer a one-way handoff of goods; it's a partnership of insight and innovation. In the semiconductor world, this might mean collaborating directly with customers on custom ASICs (Application-Specific Integrated Circuits), packaging requirements, or supply assurance models. The goal? Build exactly what the customer needs—nothing more, nothing less—while strengthening trust and locking in long-term loyalty.

Think of Apple's long-standing collaboration with TSMC. Apple doesn't just place a PO and wait—it co-engineers next-gen chips, influences roadmap decisions, and shares demand signals far in advance to secure wafer starts. The result? Market-leading performance, priority access, and fewer surprises. That's not just good business—it's culinary synergy.

Co-creation can take many forms: design sprints with key accounts, supplier innovation forums, or real-time planning sessions using shared digital platforms. Some companies even embed customer teams within their product development groups, ensuring feedback isn't just heard—it's baked in from the start. It's like inviting your most loyal diners into the kitchen to test sauces and sample reductions.

Technology plays a vital role here. Collaborative PLM platforms, cloud-based portals, and AI-enhanced feedback loops allow for rapid iteration and alignment. One EMS (Electronics Manufacturing Services) provider implemented a "virtual kitchen"—a digital environment where enterprise customers could test BOM changes, simulate outcomes, and approve configurations without a single in-person meeting. The results? A 40% reduction in design revisions and faster time to market.

But co-creation also requires cultural readiness. You can't just hand over the spatula to every guest; you need structure, transparency, and a shared language. That means defining roles, timelines, and expectations clearly. It also means being open to critique, flexible in your process, and willing to share both the glory and the grind.

When done right, co-creation isn't chaotic—it's collaborative choreography. It turns the customer into a creative partner and makes the final product more relevant, more valuable, and more resilient to change. In a world where speed, customization, and differentiation reign, co-creation might just be your tastiest competitive edge.

Collaborative Planning: When Chefs and Diners Sync Their Calendars

Imagine a chef and a guest designing a tasting menu together—not just for tonight, but for the whole year. They talk about seasonality, sourcing, dietary needs, and the timing of special occasions. That's what collaborative planning feels like in a modern supply chain: a strategic conversation between producer and consumer, focused on syncing capacity with demand and agility with insight.

In traditional supply chains, planning is often a solitary activity—each player operating in their own silo. But as customization becomes king, siloed planning breaks down like an overworked emulsification. Collaborative planning brings everyone to the same table—suppliers, customers, logistics providers, and even design and marketing teams—so that no one is working off outdated assumptions or serving a course no one ordered.

In the semiconductor world, this becomes critical. Lead times are long, capacity is finite, and demand can spike with little warning. That's why companies like AMD, NVIDIA, and Qualcomm engage in Sales and Operations Planning (S&OP) with key foundry and packaging partners. They share forecasts, adjust production timelines, and even align R&D priorities—all so that wafer starts and die sizes match customer needs at the right moment. It's the difference between overcooking inventory and nailing the service window.

Collaborative planning tools today are like the digital equivalent of a shared mise en place board. Cloud-based IBP (Integrated Business Planning) platforms allow real-time data sharing, demand shaping, scenario modeling, and constraint visibility across the ecosystem. These platforms turn forecasting into a living recipe—updated, refined, and rebalanced in response to new data, new constraints, and fresh customer feedback.

But it's not just about systems—it's about mindset. True collaboration means being transparent about limitations, open to feedback, and ready to pivot. It means surfacing issues early—whether that's a shortage of raw materials or a marketing campaign that's outpacing inventory—and solving them together. Like chefs coordinating plating times, each player must understand their timing, their tools, and the expectations of the next person down the line.

The payoff? Reduced stockouts, smoother product launches, and fewer costly surprises. And, more importantly, a stronger sense of partnership—the kind that keeps customers coming back not just for what you make, but for how you make it.

Serving Up Personalization with Precision

Customization is no longer a luxury—it's the new standard. From à la carte options to co-created products, the modern supply chain is expected to deliver flavor, flexibility, and finesse in every order. Like a chef fine-tuning a dish to each guest's palate, today's supply chain leaders must adapt recipes, timing, and plating to meet a kaleidoscope of expectations.

This chapter showed us how personalization is not just a trend—it's a full-service strategy. From flexible manufacturing and segmentation to co-creation and collaborative planning, the goal is clear: deliver the right experience at the right time, in the right way.

8

BALANCING SWEET AND SAVORY – FINANCIAL MANAGEMENT IN SUPPLY CHAINS

Cost Recipes: Breaking Down the Bill of Materials

EVERY DISH STARTS WITH INGREDIENTS, but the best chefs also know the **cost per plate**. They weigh the price of saffron against its flavor payoff, the value of prime cuts over cheaper alternatives, and the shelf life of perishables that could go to waste. Supply chains are no different. In a world where margins are lean and volatility simmers constantly on the back burner, **financial management is about balancing bold flavor with fiscal restraint**.

Enter the **Bill of Materials (BOM)**—our kitchen's master recipe. In the supply chain, the BOM is more than just a list; it's a financial blueprint. Each line item, from capacitors to connectors, contributes to the final cost of a semiconductor or finished good. Like a chef itemizing costs from truffle oil to microgreens, procurement and operations leaders must know which components are driving costs, which can be substituted, and which offer the best value per function.

Let's use a real-world wafer example: a logic chip used in automotive ECUs (Engine Control Unit). The silicon die might account for 45% of the total BOM cost, while packaging and testing make up another 30%, and passive components and substrates round out the rest. But during a supply shortage, even a humble $0.12 capacitor can become the bottleneck that halts a $300 ECU from shipping. That's the equivalent of running out of parsley and being unable to serve the risotto. **Financial oversight must be both granular and strategic.**

And it's not just about unit price—it's about **total cost of ownership (TCO)**. Some ingredients may look cheap up front but bring hidden costs—higher failure rates, longer lead times, import tariffs, or expensive logistics. That's why sophisticated supply chains factor in landed cost analysis, supplier payment terms, yield reliability, and return logistics when evaluating sourcing decisions. A sweet deal today might sour the margins tomorrow.

In the semiconductor industry, this becomes especially nuanced when fab capacity and yield rates directly affect profitability. If one packaging partner achieves 98% yield but charges a premium, while another hits 92% at a discount, the true cost is more complex than price tags alone. **It's like choosing between a skilled sous-chef and a cheaper trainee—the wrong call could ruin the dish.**

By building cost models that are dynamic, transparent, and aligned across departments—from engineering to finance—companies gain clarity and agility. They can simulate the impact of price increases, shortages, or design changes before those ingredients ever hit the line. And when it comes time to cook, they know not only the recipe but also what each spoonful costs.

Budgeting for the Banquet - Strategic Financial Planning Across the Value Chain

In a Michelin-starred kitchen, planning a banquet isn't just about what's going on the plate—it's about **reserving ingredients, aligning prep across teams, coordinating timing, and calculating every ounce of waste and cost**. The same logic applies in supply chains. Strategic financial planning isn't just a budgeting exercise—it's the mise en place of a globally orchestrated feast.

At the core is **Sales and Operations Planning (S&OP)**—the culinary calendar that aligns demand forecasts, supply capabilities, and financial goals. It's like syncing the front of house and back of house: Sales promises a full reservation book, but Finance needs to know if the kitchen can deliver without overstocking ingredients or hiring too many hands. When this collaboration hums, the result is a balanced meal with no spoiled inventory, no missed revenue, and no bitter aftertaste of cost overruns.

In the semiconductor world, where lead times can stretch 16–26 weeks and capacity is often constrained, financial planning means committing capital early, intelligently, and with risk in mind. Should we lock in long-term wafer capacity now at premium rates? Should we invest in buffer inventory for volatile SKUs? Should we delay tooling for a product line that's still unconfirmed? These are the tough menu calls—the foie gras vs. farm-to-table chicken of capital planning.

Strategic financial planning also involves **scenario modeling**. Much like a head chef must adapt the menu to seasonal availability or sudden price hikes (think: wild mushrooms after a dry spring), supply chain leaders must prepare for fluctuating demand, geopolitical shifts, and currency swings. Tools like rolling forecasts, zero-based budgeting, and digital twins let you simulate outcomes before committing to the recipe. And that saves both your budget and your bacon.

Let's not forget **interdepartmental alignment**. Finance doesn't operate in a vacuum; their spreadsheets must sync with procurement's contracts, engineering's BOMs, and operations' lead time constraints. If one team's assumptions are off—even by a pinch—the entire financial flavor can turn. Think of it like a salt-heavy sauce: it only takes one misstep to throw the dish off.

Global examples abound. **ASML**, the Dutch leader in photolithography systems, forecasts demand and secures supply years in advance, aligning long-horizon capital spending with customer roadmaps and supplier capabilities. Meanwhile, **Samsung Electronics** builds modularity into its planning to pivot resources across DRAM,

NAND, and logic divisions depending on market heat—like a chef redirecting ingredients from a banquet to à la carte as needed.

Cash Flow Cuisine - Managing Liquidity Without Burning the Sauce

Imagine running a kitchen with no cash in the drawer. You've got ingredients on order, staff on the clock, and customers waiting—but you can't pay for today's delivery or cover payroll by Friday. That's what poor liquidity management feels like in the supply chain: a recipe with all the right ingredients but no heat to bring it together.

Cash flow is the lifeblood of any supply chain—more delicate than a beurre blanc and just as easy to break. It's not simply about profit and loss; it's about **timing, velocity, and working capital discipline**. In a semiconductor operation, where equipment purchases can reach into the hundreds of millions and lead times stretch months or years, liquidity must be handled with the same precision as wafer alignment.

At the heart of liquidity management is the **cash conversion cycle**—the time it takes to convert inventory investments into cash from customers. Shortening this cycle is like trimming prep time in the kitchen. The faster you turn over ingredients (inventory), the sooner you serve the meal (sales) and collect the bill (receivables). Techniques like Vendor-managed inventory (VMI), just-in-time (JIT) delivery, and dynamic discounting for early payments help accelerate flow and free up working capital.

But it's a balancing act. Pushing too hard on payment terms with suppliers can strain relationships or jeopardize supply reliability—like sending your fishmonger home unpaid and expecting a fresh delivery tomorrow. Conversely, overstocking to avoid disruption can freeze millions in idle inventory, just like prepping 200 soufflés with no reservations on the books.

In the global semiconductor arena, liquidity management often requires navigating foreign exchange risks, customs pre-payments, and massive capex commitments. For example, a fab expansion project may require phased capital allocation over quarters or years. Teams must model cash outlays against ramp schedules and customer commitments, ensuring liquidity doesn't evaporate mid-build—like running out of gas halfway through a 12-hour braise.

Companies like **Texas Instruments** are renowned for managing inventory tightly while still maintaining customer reliability. Their fab-light model balances internal and external production while avoiding unnecessary overcommitments. On the other side, **Tesla's supplier payment model** includes tight terms offset by large volume promises —allowing it to preserve cash even as it scales aggressively.

Managing liquidity isn't glamorous. It doesn't have the flair of strategy or the spotlight of innovation. But it is the simmer behind the scenes that keeps the dish alive. And when done right, it enables you to invest in bold moves, respond to emergencies, and season your operations just right.

Profitability by the Plate - Costing, Pricing, and Margin Mastery in the Supply Chain Bistro

Behind every stunning plate of food is a balancing act between taste and cost. A pinch too much saffron or a drizzle of imported truffle oil can push a dish from profitable to painful. The same is true in supply chains: profitability isn't just about pushing volume—it's about **mastering the margins**.

Costing in the supply chain is like recipe costing in a restaurant. You start with your **bill of materials**, layer on **labor, logistics, overhead**, and finally season with **risk buffers** and **quality controls**. But unlike a static recipe, these inputs are in constant motion—affected by raw material prices, labor availability, energy costs, and market demand. In semiconductors, for instance, pricing can fluctuate wildly with foundry capacity and silicon shortages. It's the difference between plating a standard risotto and having to adjust mid-service because the arborio ran out.

Smart financial chefs constantly monitor their **ingredient costs** (component pricing), their **prep processes** (conversion costs), and their **final presentation** (customer pricing strategies). Tools like **activity-based costing (ABC)** allow operations teams to understand which products or services drive value and which are bleeding margins. For example, a low-volume, high-mix assembly might consume more test time, more specialized tooling, and more engineering support than a high-volume runner—but if priced as a standard product, it could become a silent margin killer.

That's where **cost-to-serve analysis** comes in. It's like knowing that the flambé you make tableside costs more in labor, insurance, and training—and deciding whether the flair justifies the expense. In semiconductor supply chains, this means asking: does the customer requiring 72-hour turnarounds and six layers of documentation actually deliver enough revenue to justify the service level?

On the pricing side, too many companies set it and forget it. But just like seasonal menus, **pricing should flex with the market**, the customer segment, and even the stage of the product lifecycle. Early-stage products might carry premium margins due to scarcity and innovation. But as volume ramps up and competition enters, pricing strategies should adjust accordingly—just like a restaurant discounts end-of-day pastries.

Margin mastery also involves **negotiating smarter contracts**, **standardizing procurement**, and **engaging in value engineering** to trim unnecessary costs while preserving function. Think of it like substituting ingredients without compromising flavor—can you swap that rare, imported mushroom for a local varietal and still wow the diner?

The ultimate goal is not just to make a dish profitable once—but to build a menu (product portfolio) that sustains profitability over time, across markets, and through supply chain volatility. It's not enough to serve; you need to serve smart.

Budgeting the Banquet - Strategic Planning and Investment for Sustainable Supply Chains

In any great kitchen, planning a banquet isn't just about choosing the dishes—it's about understanding the cost, timing, and return on every element that lands on the plate. The same holds true in supply chains. Strategic financial planning is the mise en place of long-term success—quietly powering decisions that determine whether an operation can scale like a holiday feast or burn out before the appetizers are served.

For semiconductor operations, this becomes even more critical. We're not just talking about stocking up on flour and eggs; we're managing multimillion-dollar equipment, global logistics flows, wafer pricing volatility, and long-term supplier investments. Financial discipline and forward planning transform a good supply chain into a competitive weapon. Think of it as the budgeting version of a banquet menu—balancing indulgent offerings with operational efficiency to deliver satisfaction without overstuffing the margins.

Just as a head chef balances cost per dish with culinary impact, supply chain leaders must consider capital expenditures versus operational expenditures (CapEx vs. OpEx). Should you invest in a new packaging line or outsource to an OSAT partner? Will that shiny automation tool reduce labor costs and improve cycle time, or is it an unnecessary garnish? These aren't just tactical questions—they're strategic decisions that shape the financial health of your entire enterprise.

One high-impact technique is **should-cost modeling**. It's like deconstructing a complex recipe to understand the cost of each ingredient, down to the gram. In the supply chain world, that means breaking down supplier quotes into raw materials, labor, overhead, and margin—so you're not just accepting a price; you're challenging it with data-backed insight. A fabless semiconductor firm in Singapore used this method to renegotiate substrate contracts, saving $2.5 million annually by revealing supplier markups on copper that were double the market rate.

Scenario planning is another key tool in the budget chef's toolkit. Just like planning for dietary restrictions or a sudden influx of guests, supply chain finance must account for volatility—currency swings, market slumps, or unexpected surges in demand. Dynamic financial modeling helps you build flexible forecasts that can adapt quickly, allowing you to reallocate resources without sacrificing service. Consider it a financial mise en place everything prepped and portioned, ready for action.

And then there's sustainability—the financial equivalent of sourcing organic and reducing waste. Investors, customers, and governments are now demanding responsible, eco-conscious practices. But sustainability isn't just a trend—it's a smart investment. Companies that reduce carbon footprints, optimize energy use, and design circular supply chains often discover new efficiencies that drop straight to the bottom line. In 2022, a leading wafer manufacturer in the U.S. invested in closed-loop water systems and saw a 12% reduction in operating costs over two years.

Ultimately, strategic financial planning is about creating a kitchen that can serve more than one dish at a time. It's about investing wisely, anticipating future needs, and building resilience that can stand the test of market shifts and material shortages. Like a master chef who knows how to stretch a truffle across three courses without sacrificing flavor, today's supply chain leaders must balance prudence with innovation and cost with capability.

Because at the end of the day, if you don't plan your banquet budget wisely, you may find yourself out of caviar—and customers—before dessert is even plated.

Measuring the Mix - Financial KPIs That Matter Most

In the kitchen, you don't just guess if the dish is done—you taste, check the temperature, plate with precision, and, if you're serious, listen for that subtle sizzle that tells you it's just right. The same attention to detail applies to financial management in the supply chain. You can't improve what you don't measure, and the wrong mix of financial indicators can leave your operation bland or disastrously over-seasoned.

Financial Key Performance Indicators (KPIs) are the flavor gauges of your supply chain. They tell you whether the operation is savory and profitable—or if it's quietly spoiling under the heat of inefficiency. And just as no chef relies on one sense alone, no supply chain leader should rely on a single metric. It's the mix that matters.

Let's start with **Cost of Goods Sold (COGS)**—the protein of your financial stew. COGS measures the direct costs of producing the goods you sell, including materials, labor, and overhead. In semiconductor operations, this could mean wafer fabrication, testing, packaging, and shipping. A sudden spike in COGS might indicate rising raw material costs or unexpected yield losses. Like noticing your steak has been overcooked, it's your cue to investigate upstream.

Inventory Turnover is another foundational KPI—the freshness index of your pantry. It measures how quickly you're cycling through stock. Too slow? You're wasting space and tying up capital. Too fast? You might be understocking and risking shortages. One global chip supplier used inventory turnover analytics to fine-tune buffer stock levels across four continents, freeing up $9 million in working capital without compromising service.

Next is **Days Payable Outstanding (DPO)**—a measure of how long you take to pay suppliers. Stretching DPO improves short-term cash flow, but push it too far and you risk damaging supplier relationships —like keeping your fishmonger waiting too long and ending up with the less-than-fresh catch. Semiconductor leaders balance DPO with supplier engagement, sometimes offering early payments in exchange for discounts or priority allocations.

Then we have **Contribution Margin**—the financial flavor enhancer that shows how much profit each product brings in after variable costs. It helps you determine which dishes on your menu (or which SKUs in your portfolio) are the most profitable. If your high-volume chip brings razor-thin margins but your specialty sensor has a juicy spread, maybe it's time to elevate the latter to "signature" status.

And don't forget **Return on Invested Capital (ROIC)**—the measure of how well your investments are cooking. Whether you're pouring money into a new wafer fab or a warehouse automation upgrade, ROIC helps you understand if the investment is actually delivering value or just burning your budget.

Finally, **cash-to-cash cycle time** is the full-service clock: how long it takes from paying for inputs to receiving payment from customers. It's the ultimate indicator of liquidity and agility. Shortening that cycle means you're serving dishes faster, collecting the bill quicker, and freeing up capital to reinvest in innovation—or the next course.

Each KPI has its place in the kitchen. Use them in harmony, and you'll understand the true flavor profile of your supply chain. Ignore them—or obsess over the wrong ones—and you may end up seasoning your financials with guesswork instead of insight.

So grab your tasting spoons, open the dashboard, and start refining your mix. Because in the high-stakes kitchen of global operations, measuring isn't just accounting—it's artistry.

The Financial Discipline Behind Great Execution

In the culinary world, it's not just how you cook—it's how you finish that counts. The final garnish, the drizzle of aged balsamic, the plate wiped clean at the edge—these small, deliberate acts signal a mastery of discipline and care. In supply chain financial management, finishing with flair means executing with precision, accountability, and strategic foresight. It's the difference between a good quarter and a sustainable legacy.

Financial discipline isn't about penny-pinching or squeezing every last cent from the operation until it cracks. It's about knowing when to reduce the flame and when to flambé. It's about understanding your cost structure deeply—where your dollars are tied up, how your cash flows, and which investments actually deliver ROI. The most successful global supply chain leaders aren't the ones with the biggest budgets—they're the ones who manage every dollar with intention, just like a chef selects every ingredient with purpose.

Take, for example, a semiconductor fab planning a $200 million capacity expansion. Without disciplined financial modeling, it's easy to overshoot—building capacity for demand that never arrives or, worse, underinvesting and losing market share. But with strong cost-benefit analysis, scenario planning, and staged investment reviews, the fab can scale with confidence. Financial finesse, not financial firepower, makes the real difference.

The same applies to working capital. Letting inventory pile up "just in case" is like prepping 100 soufflés for a dinner party of ten—it drains space, ties up funds, and ultimately risks spoilage. Instead, real-time visibility, lean inventory strategies, and agile procurement practices ensure that capital stays as fluid as a well-tempered chocolate glaze—always ready to be poured into growth opportunities.

Then there's the human factor: financial discipline empowers teams across functions to make smarter choices. When engineers understand the cost impact of design decisions, or when buyers grasp the cash implications of payment terms, the entire organization starts cooking from the same recipe. It builds a culture where every layer—from raw materials to final delivery—reflects fiscal mindfulness without stifling innovation.

Great execution isn't born from chance—it's plated with care, timed with precision, and served with financial grace. From strategic sourcing and spend analytics to capital allocation and margin optimization, financial management is the sauce that holds the operation together.

As we wrap up this chapter, remember: supply chain finance is not just a backend task. It's a front-of-house performance. It's how you keep the kitchen open, the service flowing, and the reviews glowing.

Bon appétit to the art of managing costs, balancing value, and executing with culinary-level excellence.

9

PLATING PERFECTION – PRESENTING INSIGHTS

The Art of Presentation: Turning Raw Data into Digestible Insights

IN THE KITCHEN, no matter how exquisite the flavors or rare the ingredients, a dish isn't complete until it's plated. Presentation is more than just flair—it's the bridge between intention and experience. In the world of supply chain management, insight is our signature dish, and data is our ingredient list. But raw data, like raw dough, needs skill, timing, and finesse to become something truly memorable.

Supply chain professionals are no longer judged solely on operations alone—we're storytellers now. We need to take complex, interconnected datasets—on lead times, cost variance, supplier performance, and forecast accuracy—and transform them into a visual, digestible narrative that decision-makers can understand and act upon. That's the art of "plating perfection" in our domain.

Dashboards are our plating tools. Think of Power BI, Tableau, or QlikView as the culinary tongs and tweezers that arrange components just so. When used thoughtfully, they highlight trends, spotlight bottlenecks, and bring performance metrics to life in ways that Excel alone never could. It's the difference between serving soup in a bowl or splashing it in a bucket—presentation frames perception.

Let's say your procurement team has slashed sourcing costs by 8%, increased dual-sourcing coverage by 20%, and improved on-time delivery. Great. But if the exec team sees only a spreadsheet of scattered numbers, the impact is lost. Instead, visualize it: a time-lapse trendline, a heat map of supplier geographies, a waterfall chart of cost savings by initiative. These aren't just graphs—they're storytelling devices.

In semiconductor manufacturing, where product cycles are short and product margins tight, the ability to synthesize and present insights quickly can mean the difference between capitalizing on an emerging demand spike or missing the window altogether. Just as chefs rely on plating to elevate the diner's experience, supply chain leaders must use data storytelling to elevate the business conversation.

But here's the catch: don't over-garnish. Too many metrics, too much jargon, or overly complex visuals clutter the message. Like an over-styled plate, they distract from the main course. Keep it clean, focused, and tied to business outcomes. Answer the "So what?" before anyone asks.

In this chapter, we'll dive into the techniques that turn operational data into boardroom-ready insight—from visual storytelling and KPI alignment to tailoring content for your audience. Because in the end, it's not just what you know; it's how you serve it.

Visual Storytelling: Making Metrics Memorable

You've trimmed the costs, optimized the routes, and improved supplier performance—but if you can't tell the story with clarity and impact, you've missed the final flourish. In the same way a chef doesn't just slop ingredients onto a plate, a supply chain leader shouldn't dump a stack of charts into a PowerPoint. Data without narrative is like flavor without texture—forgettable.

Visual storytelling is the art of turning metrics into momentum. It means presenting numbers not just as figures, but as scenes—each with a beginning, a conflict, a resolution, and a takeaway. Like a tasting menu, your visuals should guide the audience through a sensory and strategic journey: What's the context? What's the tension? What did we uncover? What action should we take?

Start with a strong focal point. Just as a plated dish has a visual anchor —perhaps a glazed duck breast or a perfectly torched scallop—your report needs a lead visual that draws attention. Maybe it's a trend line showing the post-pandemic recovery of lead times, or a comparative bar chart illustrating how supplier consolidation trimmed costs by 12%. Either way, the viewer should "get it" in under five seconds.

Semiconductor supply chains, with their high complexity and rapid shifts, offer fertile ground for dynamic storytelling. Imagine a dashboard where yield loss patterns are animated over time, or where inventory turnover is color-coded by product family across global fabs. These techniques allow teams to spot issues faster, link root causes across functions, and prioritize where to dig deeper. It's the difference between reading a recipe and watching a cooking demo.

But effective storytelling goes beyond beauty—it requires relevance. Tailor the presentation to your audience. Executives want high-level outcomes and risk exposure. Engineers want root causes and process flow. Planners want demand trends and supplier fill rates. A good storyteller, like a good chef, knows their guests and adapts the meal to suit the palate.

Don't forget emotion. Even in the B2B world, great stories resonate because they matter. Instead of saying, "Backlog increased 18%, say, "Our backlog grew 18%, risking $22M in delayed revenue—unless we fast-track Supplier X's ramp by September." Now, there's urgency. Now, there's flavor.

Ultimately, your goal is to make the metrics memorable—not just for applause, but for action. When people remember what they saw, they talk about it. When they talk about it, they do something about it. And when they act, your supply chain gets stronger.

Tailoring the Message for the Right Audience

Just as a master chef wouldn't serve foie gras to a table of vegans or spice a dish for diners expecting something mild, a great supply chain communicator knows their audience. Data without context is like over-seasoned food—it might be technically correct, but it leaves a bad taste. Tailoring your message is the art of matching the insight to the eater—serving up the right flavor, in the right format, at just the right moment.

In the global kitchen of the semiconductor supply chain, your stakeholders come with wildly different palates. Executives crave clarity and strategic impact. They want to know: "Are we profitable? Where are the risks? How do we compare to last quarter?" They prefer their data like a tasting menu—elegant, concise, and easy to digest. A single KPI dashboard that shows cash-to-cash cycle time, inventory turns, and service level can tell them everything they need to know at a glance. Use clear visuals, bold trendlines, and minimal text. Leave the garnish, but hold the "garnish-on-the-garnish."

Meanwhile, your operations team wants substance. They're in the kitchen, sleeves rolled up, and they need granular detail. Give them root cause analysis, lead time variability, and fill rate trends by SKU. These stakeholders are more like prep chefs—they thrive on structure, want everything labeled, and need the data to help them cut faster and smarter. Here, layered dashboards, filterable views, and supporting tables can make all the difference.

Then there are the engineers and planners—the R&D chefs and line cooks. These folks love a good process map, control chart, or failure mode analysis. They need cause-and-effect logic, diagnostic signals, and insight that fuels continuous improvement. Serve them spreadsheets, yes—but do it with intention. Color coding, conditional formatting, and built-in commentary help them spot what matters and move quickly.

And don't forget external stakeholders—suppliers, customers, regulators. These guests aren't in your kitchen every day, so they need extra context. Supply timelines, service-level agreements, or quality dashboards should be simple, visual, and supported with commentary. Think of this as takeout: the packaging matters as much as the product inside.

One powerful strategy is to create a "data tasting flight"—the same core insights presented three ways: an executive summary, a technical appendix, and a narrative email with key callouts. This gives everyone what they need without watering down the message. It respects their time and gets results faster.

In the end, tailoring your message isn't just about formatting—it's about respect. It's about knowing who's at the table, what they're hungry for, and how to serve it in a way that satisfies. When your message hits the mark, decisions get made, actions follow, and your entire supply chain hums like a perfectly tuned kitchen brigade.

Turning Insight into Action - Driving Decisions Through Data

Presenting data is one thing—getting someone to do something with it is another. In the same way that plating a dish isn't just about aesthetics but about inviting someone to dive in, your supply chain insights must be crafted to compel action. Otherwise, they're just beautifully arranged ingredients sitting cold on the pass.

In the semiconductor world, time is not just money—it's innovation. A delay in decision-making can mean missed production windows, lost revenue, or a slip in competitive advantage. That's why transforming insight into action is the true purpose of supply chain reporting. You're not here to present a report card; you're here to ignite change.

Think of every insight as a call to cook. A spike in expedited freight costs isn't just a number—it's a sign that forecasting is off or that a supplier is struggling to meet lead times. A dip in inventory turns isn't just a ratio—it might point to product obsolescence, planning inaccuracies, or overly cautious buffers. Just like a chef doesn't ignore a smoking pan, a supply chain leader must jump into action the moment the data starts to sizzle.

But how do we ensure data doesn't just inform—it transforms?

First, tie every insight to a clear outcome. Don't just show the trend—translate it into implications. "This backlog in incoming inspection delayed two builds this week and cost $380K in potential revenue." Action begins when the consequence is understood.

Second, give your audience the tools to act. Include recommended next steps, escalation paths, or predefined playbooks. Use conditional formatting to highlight where thresholds are exceeded, or embed live action buttons in digital dashboards for reordering, reporting, or communication. This isn't just a report—it's a launchpad.

Third, reinforce accountability. If each report comes with clear ownership—who is driving the follow-up, when is it due, what will be measured—it stops being passive information and starts being a dynamic tool. This is mise en place at the organizational level: every role prepared, every tool sharpened, every station ready to go.

Let's not forget agility. In semiconductor manufacturing, demand shifts, geopolitical tensions, and yield issues can arise overnight. That means your insights must fuel decisions at the speed of reality. Waiting for a weekly or monthly review is like checking if the steak is done after it's been served—it's too late. Real-time dashboards, mobile-enabled alerts, and automated flags ensure the team reacts during the heat—not after the smoke clears.

The end goal? A culture where insights are expected, valued, and acted upon. Where the data is respected not for its volume, but for its velocity. Where decision-making becomes as fast, fluid, and fearless as a kitchen during peak service.

Because when insights drive action and action drives improvement, your supply chain doesn't just run—it performs.

The Presentation Pass - Delivering Data Like a Chef Delivers a Dish

In every high-end kitchen, there's a moment of truth known as the pass. It's the final checkpoint where the chef inspects the plate before it heads to the diner. Every smear of sauce, every garnish, every degree of doneness is scrutinized. Because no matter how brilliant the recipe or precise the cook, the presentation is what makes the first impression —and often determines whether the dish delights or disappoints.

In the world of supply chain, your presentation pass is how you deliver your insights. It's not just about what you're reporting—it's how you serve it. Because even the juiciest data can fall flat if it's poorly plated.

We've all seen it: dense spreadsheets, unstructured decks, dashboards with 50 KPIs and no clear message. That's like serving a five-course meal on a cafeteria tray. When you're presenting to executives, functional leaders, or global teams, you're not just sharing metrics—you're telling a story with stakes, tension, and a clear call to action.

First, choose your plate wisely. Match the format to the audience. Executives want high-level summaries and bottom-line impact—fast. Ops managers need granularity and control levers. Engineers are looking for root cause narratives. Don't give the same plate to every diner. Curate the meal.

Second, think about flavor pacing. Lead with the key insight, not the raw data. Hook your audience with the "why it matters" before diving into the "how we got here." Use analogies, benchmarks, or real-world comparisons—don't just drop numbers. Just as a chef layers textures and temperatures, layer your message for engagement.

Third, garnish with design. Clean visuals, color coding, smart data grouping—all of it helps the audience digest complex insights faster. A thoughtful chart can speak louder than a thousand rows of data. Remember: simplicity isn't about dumbing down; it's about elevating clarity.

And finally, own the pass. Present with confidence, energy, and relevance. Be ready for questions. Anticipate resistance. And most importantly—know the ingredients of your report inside and out. Like a chef who can explain every herb in a reduction, you should be able to walk through every data point with clarity and authority.

When done right, the presentation pass isn't a formality—it's your moment to influence, align, and inspire action. It's where trust is built, credibility is plated, and momentum is served.

Because, in the end, insights that aren't delivered with precision, clarity, and flair are just ingredients left unassembled. But those that are—those delivered like a perfectly plated dish—can change the course of your supply chain.

10

THE TASTE TEST - PERFORMANCE METRICS

The First Bite: Why Metrics Matter More Than You Think

IN THE CULINARY WORLD, the first bite tells you everything. It's the moment of truth—where intention meets execution, and the dish either sings or sinks. The flavors, the textures, the temperature—each element silently whispers how well the kitchen performed. In the supply chain world, performance metrics are that first bite. They reveal not only what's been done, but how well it was done, where things are trending, and whether your operation is ready to serve another round.

Metrics aren't just fancy garnishes on executive dashboards—they're the taste test of your supply chain's discipline, agility, and quality. The right metrics guide decision-making, surface inefficiencies, and align teams. The wrong ones? They clutter the plate, distract from the main course, and can mislead stakeholders into complacency or chaos.

In semiconductor operations, where every nanosecond and nanometer counts, performance measurement becomes especially critical. Imagine trying to run a cleanroom without yield metrics, cycle time data, or tool utilization rates—it would be like cooking in the dark with no idea if your oven is even on. Metrics light the path. They show where things are flowing, where they're stuck, and where adjustments are needed—whether that's optimizing a supplier's on-time delivery or pinpointing a bottleneck on a wafer line.

But not all metrics carry equal weight. Some are appetizers—nice to have but not filling. Others are entrées—core to how you manage cost, quality, and service. It's about knowing what to measure, why you're measuring it, and how those results align with your overall goals. A chef wouldn't judge a dish only by its plating; they'd taste it, test its texture, and smell the seasoning. Likewise, your supply chain KPIs must reflect the full flavor profile of performance.

For example, on-time delivery may be the gold standard for customer satisfaction—but if it's achieved at the expense of inventory bloat or expedited shipping chaos, then the taste test fails. Likewise, hitting cost targets without tracking quality metrics might save money short-term but could poison customer trust in the long run.

That's why modern supply chains need a balanced scorecard—one that captures flavor, texture, aroma, and presentation. A well-rounded set of KPIs blends operational efficiency (like inventory turns and asset utilization) with customer-facing outcomes (like fill rate and response time) and strategic foresight (such as forecast accuracy or supply risk exposure).

In this chapter, we'll sharpen our palate to explore the metrics that matter most—how to select them, refine them, and use them to season your decisions. Because in the end, just like the finest dishes, your supply chain will always be judged by the result on the plate.

Core KPIs - What Every Supply Chain Should Be Tracking

In the fast-paced kitchen of supply chain operations, your KPIs are the mise en place of performance—your key ingredients laid out and ready for the heat of execution. Just as a chef relies on critical checkpoints like internal temperature, cook time, and plating symmetry to deliver culinary perfection, a well-run supply chain lives and breathes by its core Key Performance Indicators (KPIs). Without them, you're cooking blind and hoping for a miracle.

Let's start with a few essentials that belong in every supply chain's pantry.

1. On-Time Delivery (OTD): This is your "dish out of the kitchen" moment. It measures how reliably you meet your customer's expectations—on time, in full, without surprises. Whether you're shipping wafers, wire harnesses, or wafer-handling robots, OTD is the first metric your customers notice. In semiconductor operations, where production windows are tight and lines run 24/7, even a 1-day slip can mean weeks of lost yield downstream. OTD doesn't just reflect logistics—it's the culmination of everything from procurement planning to supplier performance to internal alignment.

2. Inventory Turnover: Think of this like your walk-in fridge—you don't want ingredients lingering too long. Inventory turnover tells you how efficiently you're using working capital and how well your demand planning aligns with your replenishment strategy. Too low, and you risk obsolescence (or moldy produce); too high, and you're constantly running out of stock (and scrambling for substitutes).

3. Order Accuracy & Fill Rate: These are the plating metrics—did you serve what was ordered, complete, and without missing garnishes? In high-mix semiconductor environments, where one wrong part can halt production, order accuracy becomes non-negotiable. Fill rate, on the other hand, tells you what percent of customer demand you're able to meet without delay or backorder. Together, they reveal whether your supply chain is serving reliably or fumbling the handoff.

4. Forecast Accuracy: Forecasting is like preheating the oven—you have to start with the right temperature, or the entire recipe gets skewed. Forecast accuracy measures how close your predicted demand aligns with actual consumption. It's especially critical in volatile markets like semiconductors, where demand can spike or plummet based on macroeconomic shifts, consumer trends, or new tech launches.

5. Supply Chain Cycle Time: This KPI tracks the time it takes to turn a customer order into a delivered product. Like cooking time, it reflects both speed and consistency. The goal isn't just to move fast—it's to move smart. You want predictable, repeatable processes that shorten cycle time without compromising quality.

6. Quality Metrics (like FPY, RMA, QPPM): First Pass Yield (FPY), Return Material Authorization (RMA) rates, and Quality Parts Per Million (QPPM) measure the "flavor consistency" of your operation. You can't claim a top-tier dish if it tastes different every time. The same goes for components and builds—quality drives customer trust, cost efficiency, and long-term viability.

7. Supplier Performance: Just like sourcing the freshest produce impacts the final dish, the performance of your suppliers affects every link in your chain. Are they delivering on time? Are their components meeting specifications? A great chef knows their purveyors—and great supply chain teams track supplier KPIs just as rigorously.

These KPIs aren't static—they evolve with your business. But taken together, they form the foundational scorecard that enables strategic decisions, continuous improvement, and operational excellence. It's not just about collecting data; it's about tracking the right data, interpreting the signals, and acting before the dish burns.

Next, we'll explore how to cook these numbers into something truly powerful—through benchmarking, real-time dashboards, and metric-driven alignment across your kitchen brigade.

Benchmarking for Excellence - Knowing When You've Hit the Sweet Spot

In any professional kitchen, a chef doesn't just rely on taste alone—they compare, refine, and measure their dishes against a standard. Is the risotto creamier than last night's? Is the steak perfectly seared like the competitor down the street? In supply chain management, this culinary calibration is known as "benchmarking." It's the art of knowing not just how you're performing, but how your performance stacks up against the best in class.

Benchmarking isn't about vanity metrics or chasing perfection. It's about finding your sweet spot—the balanced point where cost, speed, service, and quality intersect in harmony. Just as chefs benchmark their creations against Michelin-starred plates, supply chain leaders assess their KPIs against internal targets, industry standards, and peer competitors. The result? A sharper understanding of where excellence lives—and how to serve it consistently.

Start with internal benchmarks. These are your historical baselines. How does your current OTD compare to last quarter's? Has your inventory turnover improved year over year? Are quality metrics showing a positive trend? Internal benchmarks help you assess whether your continuous improvement programs are actually… well, improving.

But excellence requires stepping outside your own kitchen. External benchmarks take the pulse of your industry. Tools like Gartner's "Supply Chain Top 25," McKinsey's Ops Metrics, or industry-specific dashboards from associations like SEMI (for semiconductors) allow you to compare your KPIs against global leaders. If your inventory turnover is 5 and the best-in-class is 12, you know you've got room to sharpen your knives.

Of course, benchmarking isn't about copying recipes—it's about adapting best practices to fit your unique flavor. Maybe your cycle time is longer because you build highly customized products. Or perhaps your higher logistics cost is justified by a premium customer experience. The trick is knowing which metrics should be improved and which are strategic choices based on your supply chain menu.

Benchmarking also reveals blind spots. You might be hyper-focused on supplier OTD, only to realize your peers are outperforming you in forecast accuracy or cash-to-cash cycle time. These insights redirect your improvement efforts like a sommelier suggesting a better wine pairing—unexpected but transformative.

Take semiconductor giant Texas Instruments. By benchmarking their internal supply chain against industry peers, they identified opportunities to dramatically improve manufacturing cycle time and reduce lead time variability. The outcome? A more agile supply chain that outperforms rivals on responsiveness without bloating inventory.

Benchmarking, when done right, is both a mirror and a compass. It shows you who you are and guides you toward who you could be. And just like the best chefs study global trends while perfecting local flavors, world-class supply chains look outward for inspiration while staying grounded in operational truth.

The final test of a well-benchmarked KPI isn't just a higher score—it's how that metric improves decision-making, customer satisfaction, and profitability. Because, in the end, knowing where you stand is the first step toward moving forward.

Metric-Driven Culture - Getting Your Whole Team to Taste the Numbers

In any well-run kitchen, everyone—from the executive chef to the line cook—knows what "good" looks like. The doneness of a steak, the consistency of a sauce, the crisp on a crème brûlée—all are understood, monitored, and executed with consistency. Now imagine if only the sous-chef knew those standards, and the rest of the team was left to guess. Chaos, right? The same principle applies in supply chain management: metrics only matter when they're shared, understood, and embraced by the entire team.

Creating a metric-driven culture is about making performance measurable, visible, and actionable across every layer of your supply chain. It's getting your people to not just look at the numbers—but to taste them. To feel ownership over them. To treat KPIs like seasoning: constantly adjusting until the flavor—the performance—is just right.

It starts with **transparency**. In a kitchen, the pass is the central point where every dish is reviewed before it goes out. In a supply chain, that pass is your dashboard. Whether it's daily production volumes, forecast accuracy, or supplier OTD, key metrics need to be visible to everyone—from procurement to planning to logistics. Visibility breeds accountability. And just like a kitchen can't function if the grill station doesn't know when orders are spiking, your team needs real-time data to anticipate and act.

Next is **ownership**. A true metric-driven culture gives every team member a stake in the results. Planners should own forecast accuracy. Buyers should own cost variance. Suppliers should be looped into quality metrics. When each player understands their contribution to the final plate—er, product—they're more invested in getting it right. At one leading semiconductor fab, for example, integrating supplier scorecards into joint quarterly reviews led to a 15% improvement in supplier responsiveness in under a year. Why? Because the numbers weren't hidden—they were shared, celebrated, and occasionally grilled.

But metrics without context are like salt without balance—overused, and they ruin the dish. That's why **storytelling matters**. Frame metrics around customer impact. Don't just say defect rate dropped by 0.2%—show how that translated to higher yields or fewer RMAs. Instead of just tracking lead time, show how improved agility helped capture unexpected demand. Give your data a narrative, and people will remember—and act.

Finally, **celebrate the wins**. Create a recognition culture where metric improvements are toasted like a perfectly executed soufflé. Whether it's a quarterly "Golden Ladle" award for best KPI performance or a team lunch to honor a new record in cycle time reduction, celebration fuels momentum.

In a metric-driven culture, data is more than digits—it's the seasoning, the structure, and the soul of decision-making. When everyone's palate is trained to taste performance, greatness becomes repeatable. And the results? A team that not only delivers consistently but does so with pride, clarity, and a shared sense of purpose.

Metrics as Your Culinary Compass

In the end, performance metrics aren't just about tracking—they're about transforming. Like the final taste test before service, metrics tell you if your supply chain masterpiece is ready for the world or if it needs a touch more salt, a splash less vinegar, or a complete redo of the dish.

They serve as your culinary compass in an ever-shifting supply chain landscape. From core KPIs like on-time delivery and inventory turns to forward-looking metrics like forecast accuracy and supplier responsiveness, these numbers guide your every move. But more than that, they align your crew—giving planners, buyers, operators, and suppliers a shared language to collaborate, challenge, and grow.

In high-stakes environments like semiconductor manufacturing, where milliseconds and microns matter, metrics drive discipline. They flag issues before they spoil the dish and help prioritize improvement efforts where they'll have the most impact. Whether you're running a lean fab line or managing a complex global sourcing network, your metrics act as your mise en place chaos, ensuring readiness and setting the stage for excellence.

But don't forget: metrics are only as powerful as the culture behind them. Numbers that sit in isolation, buried in dashboards no one checks, are like secret recipes never tasted. To unlock their full flavor, they must be lived, shared, and savored. Turn your metrics into team mantras. Bake them into your operating rhythms. And most of all, use them not to punish—but to empower.

When your team can taste the numbers, they don't just execute—they elevate. They stop seeing metrics as mandates and start treating them as tools to sharpen, refine, and innovate. Like a perfectly plated dish, the beauty is in the balance—the harmony between data, discipline, and daily execution.

So, sharpen your knives, clear your dashboards, and keep your palate trained. Because in the kitchen of modern supply chains, metrics aren't the end of the meal—they're the recipe for repeatable success.

11

CULINARY COLLABORATION – CROSS-FUNCTIONAL TEAMS

Stirring the Pot Together – Why Collaboration is Your Secret Ingredient

EVERY GREAT KITCHEN thrives on synergy. Watch any bustling brigade de cuisine, and you'll see it: the line cook sears while the saucier stirs, the pastry chef plates while the expeditor calls the shots—all moving in harmony with the energy of a finely tuned jazz band. It's not about one superstar chef; it's about a team working from the same recipe, with the same sense of urgency and pride. That same dynamic is the lifeblood of high-functioning supply chains.

In semiconductor operations, collaboration isn't just a soft skill—it's a strategic imperative. From R&D to sourcing, from planning to manufacturing, and from logistics to customer service, each function plays a distinct yet interconnected role in delivering that final product—a wafer-thin masterpiece engineered to perfection. If even one player misses the beat, the entire flow can spiral into chaos faster than an over-salted reduction.

Cross-functional teams bring together diverse expertise, perspectives, and priorities. But like any diverse kitchen crew, they don't always speak the same language. Procurement is watching price points, planning is chasing demand curves, engineering is defending specs, and finance is slicing costs with a scalpel. Without a shared vision and collaborative rhythm, those teams can become silos—each optimizing their own dish while the full-course meal suffers.

That's where culinary collaboration becomes essential. It's about crafting a culture where departments don't just coexist—they co-create. Like a tasting table before a grand service, it involves early input, real-time feedback, and a commitment to continuous iteration. Planning invites operations to the forecast discussion. Procurement loops in engineering during supplier selection. Quality works side by side with manufacturing during NPI ramps. It's not a one-and-done conversation—it's a rolling boil of insight, challenge, and alignment.

Just ask any company that has launched a new chip platform on time and under budget—they didn't do it in isolation. They ran daily stand-ups, hosted cross-functional war rooms, and treated collaboration not as a bonus but as a baseline. Intel's NPI ramps, Nvidia's GPU launches, and AMD's fabless coordination with foundries were all made possible because departments sat at the same table, with sleeves rolled up and the end customer in mind.

In this chapter, we'll explore the tools and mindsets that foster true cross-functional excellence. From communication rituals to role clarity, from shared KPIs to decision frameworks, we'll unpack how to create alignment that sticks. Because when your kitchen crew plays as one, you don't just deliver—you delight.

Mise en Place for the Mindset" - Establishing a Culture of Collaboration

In a world-class kitchen, mise en place isn't just about chopped onions and lined-up spices—it's a mindset. It's the invisible discipline that underpins flow, teamwork, and precision. The same goes for collaboration in the supply chain. Before any product can flow seamlessly from concept to customer, organizations need to prepare their most important ingredient: a culture that values and enables cross-functional partnership.

Culture, after all, is the heat that either warms a collaborative stew or boils tensions over. Without intentional effort, even well-meaning teams default to turf wars and defensive behaviors. Procurement guards its budget, engineering digs in on specs, and planning lobs demand forecasts over the wall like a last-minute garnish. True collaboration starts with an agreement on the kitchen rules—how we work, communicate, and solve problems together.

The best organizations establish these norms through deliberate rituals and reinforced behaviors. Daily stand-ups across departments foster real-time transparency—just like a chef's pre-service huddle to review orders, call out specials, and adjust the plan. Cross-functional reviews aren't about finger-pointing—they're about flavor balancing. Did the supplier substitution impact yield? Did that last-minute ECO throw off planning? Everyone has a seat at the table, and every voice is part of the recipe.

Psychological safety is also essential mise en place. Just as a junior line cook must feel safe calling out a missing garnish before a plate leaves the pass, team members must feel empowered to raise risks, challenge assumptions, and suggest improvements without fear of retaliation. This openness breeds trust—and trust is the oil that keeps the kitchen humming.

In semiconductor supply chains, where precision is critical and innovation rapid, building this culture of collaboration pays massive dividends. TSMC, for example, doesn't just provide wafers; it co-develops platforms with customers, ensuring cross-functional alignment from the design floor to the fab. At Cisco, global supply chain war rooms bring together planners, engineers, and suppliers to solve disruptions in real time—no blame, just brisk execution.

Leaders play a key role in setting the tone. When leaders model cross-functional empathy, prioritize team goals over functional wins, and celebrate shared successes, the entire kitchen follows suit. Incentives matter too: shared KPIs, bonus structures that reward alignment, and performance reviews that include collaboration metrics can reinforce the right behaviors.

Ultimately, cultivating this mindset doesn't happen overnight—it's seasoned over time. But when it takes hold, your organization gains the ability to stir, pivot, and plate with finesse, even under pressure. Like a Michelin-starred kitchen, every hand knows its role, every voice is respected, and the final dish shines with unity.

Blending Roles and Responsibilities - Who's Stirring What Pot?

In every great kitchen, you don't see three people reaching for the same saucepan—or worse, ignoring it entirely because "it wasn't their job." Instead, you witness a seamless dance: the sous-chef chops, the line cook sears, the expediter calls the rhythm, and the dish lands on the pass exactly as imagined. That choreography isn't magic—it's the result of clearly defined roles, mutual respect, and a shared understanding of who's stirring what pot.

Cross-functional supply chain teams operate under the same principle. Without clarity, collaboration becomes chaos. But when each player understands their part in the greater recipe, things move with speed, precision, and finesse.

Let's break it down. Procurement isn't just about cutting costs; they're sourcing strategic ingredients and balancing quality and risk. Engineering isn't simply designing specs—they're anticipating manufacturability, material constraints, and supplier capabilities. Operations is optimizing the cook time and sequence, while planning ensures the oven is preheated at the right moment. Even finance has a role, stirring in the right balance of cost, investment, and return.

But roles don't mean silos. In the semiconductor world, a planner might flag a demand spike for a key node, and procurement must respond with sourcing alternatives. Engineering might need to redesign around a component shortage, and finance must reforecast spending. These handoffs need to be tight, transparent, and built on mutual accountability—not on passing the blame when the soufflé sinks.

Companies like Intel and ASML are masters at defining these collaborative swim lanes. They use responsibility assignment matrices (RACI charts) not as bureaucratic documents but as living tools—updated regularly, communicated widely, and reinforced through cadence calls and shared dashboards. It's like a kitchen station map, showing who's on hot apps, who's manning the fryers, and who's plating desserts. Everyone knows where they're stationed—and when it's time to jump in and assist.

Blending responsibilities also means embracing hybrid roles. In lean organizations, you might have a planner with procurement chops or an engineer who can speak fluently to sourcing constraints. These "culinary hybrids" bridge gaps naturally, reducing translation errors and helping teams stir the pot together.

The key is ensuring nobody overcooks the dish—or leaves it cold. When responsibilities overlap without clarity, decisions stall or duplicate efforts arise. When they're too rigid, teams fail to flex during high-pressure moments. The sweet spot lies in dynamic ownership, where roles are defined but collaboration is fluid.

By mapping responsibilities like a menu, clarifying who owns which steps, and fostering cross-training, your team becomes a high-functioning brigade—not just faster, but tastier. Everyone owns the outcome, even if their hands never touch the pan.

Communication in the Kitchen - Keeping the Pass Clear

If you've ever watched a professional kitchen during peak dinner service, you know there's no time for ambiguity. Orders fly in, dishes fly out, and every team member—from garde manger to grill station—relies on crisp, clear communication to keep the rhythm intact. The expediter at the pass barks out the next ticket, synchronizing efforts with laser focus. One muddled command, one missed "fire," and the whole service unravels like an overworked risotto.

The same principle applies to cross-functional supply chain teams. Communication isn't just helpful—it's the pass. It's the vital space where strategy becomes execution, where planning turns into production, and where problems are flagged and resolved before they burn the bottom line.

In a global semiconductor operation, where timelines are compressed and tolerance for error is razor-thin, communication must be as sharp as a chef's knife. Engineering must align with procurement on specs before RFQs go out. Operations needs real-time updates from planning to adjust production priorities. Finance must know when supplier costs rise so forecasts can be updated. This is not the place for passive-aggressive Slack messages or endless email chains that age like day-old pasta.

That's why high-performing teams embrace communication cadences as part of their mise en place. Daily stand-ups, weekly S&OP huddles, cross-functional program reviews—these aren't just meetings; they're strategic rituals. They function like pre-service check-ins in a Michelin-starred kitchen: "Are we clear on tonight's specials? Do we have enough scallops? Is the fry station ready?" Everyone aligns before the heat kicks in.

Digital collaboration platforms like Microsoft Teams, Slack, or Asana play the role of the modern kitchen's order board. But tools alone don't guarantee clarity—it's how you use them. The best teams create a shared language: flags for risks, emojis for urgency, and dashboards that speak across departments. They establish clear protocols—who owns what, when to escalate, and how to surface roadblocks early.

Silence is the enemy. In semiconductor supply chains, a single late update can cause cascading issues across fabs, subcontractors, and OEMs. If the logistics team doesn't know that customs delayed a shipment, the production line may grind to a halt. Just like a line cook who forgets to say "behind" can cause a collision, missing critical updates leads to disruption, waste, and rework.

Strong communication also includes the courage to raise a hand. Great kitchen teams speak up when something's off—too much salt in the sauce, the wrong plating sequence, or missing garnish. Likewise, in cross-functional teams, a culture of psychological safety allows employees to surface concerns without fear of blame. Because when the pass is clear and the airwaves are open, problems get solved before they spoil the service.

Ultimately, effective communication in supply chains is about keeping the path clear—so ideas, data, and feedback move swiftly, seamlessly, and in sync. When everyone knows what's cooking, you serve better, faster, and with fewer surprises.

Trust in the Team - No Micromanaging the Mise

In any great kitchen, the head chef doesn't hover behind every station, second-guessing knife technique or double-checking seasoning. They trust their team—the sous, the line cooks, the pastry lead—to handle their stations with precision and pride. Because in the heat of service, micromanaging is a recipe for disaster. It slows the flow, suffocates creativity, and communicates one dangerous message: "I don't trust you to do your job."

The same is true in supply chain operations. When cross-functional teams are treated like mere executors rather than empowered professionals, collaboration breaks down. Trust is the oil in the sauté pan—it reduces friction, prevents sticking, and keeps everything moving smoothly. Without it, you get bottlenecks, burnout, and bland results.

Trust starts with clear mise en place—not just tools and timelines, but ownership. When everyone knows their responsibilities and has the autonomy to execute, magic happens. Engineering can confidently tweak design specs to improve manufacturability, knowing procurement won't override them. Logistics can reroute shipments to avoid port delays without needing a five-level approval chain. And sourcing teams can engage with suppliers proactively, instead of waiting for direction like sous-chefs with no prep list.

At TSMC, for example, cross-disciplinary pods are empowered to make decisions on factory planning, capacity allocation, and supplier engagement. The central philosophy? Build teams that own the outcome, not just their slice of the process. In the fast-moving world of semiconductors, waiting for permission is like waiting for water to boil by staring at it—it wastes time and energy.

Micromanaging, on the other hand, signals a breakdown of trust. It clogs the flow of ideas and slows down decision-making. Team members become hesitant, defensive, and disengaged. It's like telling a line cook how to hold a knife every five minutes—they'll never grow, and your kitchen will never scale. Instead of agility, you get anxiety.

Trust also means trusting through failure. Mistakes will happen—an order gets delayed, a supplier misses the mark, or someone miscalculates demand. But if the reaction is finger-pointing and control, you squash learning and innovation. Great culinary leaders debrief, adjust, and move forward—because every burnt crust is a chance to improve the recipe.

And let's not forget the power of positive reinforcement. When trust is working, shout it out. Celebrate a planner who made the call to pivot before a shortage hit. Acknowledge the warehouse lead who streamlined inventory staging. Trust breeds confidence, and confidence breeds performance.

In the end, managing a supply chain is like running a high-end kitchen: you can't cook every dish yourself. But you can build a team that understands the flavor you're going for—and trusts each other to season it just right.

Collaboration as a Competitive Edge - From Brigade to Business Strategy

In the world of haute cuisine, a brigade isn't just a group of people—it's a synchronized system. Each role, from saucier to garde manger, plays a critical part in the kitchen's success. And when the brigade functions with harmony, the output isn't just food—it's art. The same principle applies in supply chain management: cross-functional collaboration isn't just a soft skill—it's a hard-edged strategic weapon.

When collaboration is built into your business DNA, it creates agility, innovation, and speed. In fast-paced, high-stakes industries like semiconductors, where lead times are long and stakes are higher than a soufflé on a sugar high, collaboration enables teams to pivot quickly, execute confidently, and recover with grace.

Consider this: demand planning can't work in a silo without insights from sales and market intel. Procurement can't negotiate optimal terms without input from engineering on material specs. Logistics can't optimize routes without visibility into production schedules. These interdependencies are the mise en place of modern supply chains—each function bringing their prep, timing, and technique to create a dish worthy of global delivery.

Companies like Cisco and Intel have turned collaboration into a full-fledged strategy. Cisco's S&OP (Sales and Operations Planning) process isn't just about reconciling numbers—it's a rhythm of cross-functional engagement that brings finance, marketing, engineering, and operations to the same table, making decisions together. The result? Fewer surprises, smarter inventory positions, and faster responses to disruptions. Intel's Agile Product Development cycles embed supply chain voices early in the design phase, ensuring that what is engineered is not only cutting-edge but also buildable, sourceable, and scalable. That's collaboration as a competitive advantage.

It's no longer enough to be good at your station. The real differentiator is how well your station syncs with the rest of the kitchen. That's why organizations that treat collaboration as a strategic discipline—nurturing it with the same rigor they give to metrics and margins—outperform. They have stronger supplier partnerships, faster product cycles, and more resilient operations. They turn the brigade system into a business model.

As a leader, your job isn't to bark orders from the past. It's to cultivate the conditions for collaboration: psychological safety, aligned goals, open communication, and shared wins. It's ensuring every player feels valued, heard, and empowered to contribute their unique flavor.

In the end, it's not the flashiest plating that wins the race—it's the team that preps together, pivots together, and plates with precision. Because when your brigade becomes a strategy, your supply chain becomes unbeatable.

12

SIMMERING SOLUTIONS - LEAN PRACTICES

The Lean Pantry - Trimming the Fat, Not the Flavor

IMAGINE WALKING into a restaurant kitchen where every inch of counter space is cluttered with unused gadgets, mystery ingredients are hiding in unlabeled containers, and no one knows which pan is clean. Chaos, right? Now imagine a lean kitchen—clean, organized, efficient—where every tool has a purpose and every ingredient earns its place. That's the heart of lean thinking. Not just in kitchens—but across the entire supply chain.

Lean practices aren't about cutting corners or starving your operations. They're about trimming the excess while preserving, even enhancing, the quality of what you deliver. It's the culinary equivalent of using every part of the vegetable, respecting the ingredients, and letting the flavor shine through without waste.

Originating from the Toyota Production System, lean is rooted in identifying and eliminating the seven deadly wastes—overproduction, waiting, unnecessary transport, excess inventory, overprocessing, unnecessary motion, and defects. In a semiconductor supply chain, these inefficiencies might look like too much buffer stock tying up capital, excess movement of wafers between fabs, or rework due to preventable defects. The goal? Create more value with less waste.

The trick to lean is viewing it not as a checklist, but as a mindset. Think of it like mise en place just a routine, but a discipline. It's about constantly asking, "What can we do better?" and empowering everyone in the kitchen—or the warehouse, or the assembly line—to contribute ideas. That kind of mindset shifts lean from a project to a culture.

One common misconception is that lean only works in stable, high-volume environments. But modern supply chains, particularly in fast-moving, high-mix sectors like semiconductors, prove otherwise. The most successful companies blend lean principles with agility—streamlining where they can while maintaining the flexibility to respond to market shifts. It's the supply chain equivalent of a kitchen that can turn out 100 plates of duck confit and pivot to vegan risotto when the VIP calls in a dietary request.

Tools like value stream mapping, 5S, and root cause analysis aren't just process improvement jargon—they're recipes for operational clarity. When used correctly, they help teams visualize inefficiencies, organize their space and time, and dig deep into problems rather than masking symptoms.

Ultimately, lean is about designing a supply chain that simmers steadily—no sudden boil-overs, no wasted heat. It's about creating a foundation so solid and smooth that when disruptions come—and they will—you can respond with elegance, not with an emergency.

Because in both kitchens and supply chains, excellence isn't about doing more; it's about doing better, with less.

Overcoming Resistance to Lean - When the Kitchen Pushes Back

Implementing lean practices in a supply chain can feel a lot like convincing a seasoned chef to change their signature dish. You're not just tweaking a recipe—you're challenging habits, pride, and deeply rooted ways of working. And just like in any bustling kitchen, the moment you start rearranging the spice rack or questioning why the sauce station takes up half the line, you're bound to get some pushback.

Resistance to lean isn't a sign of failure. It's a sign you're asking people to let go of something familiar. In supply chains—especially those in complex environments like semiconductor manufacturing—teams are often juggling high-stakes production schedules, compliance standards, and customer demands. Change, no matter how beneficial, can feel like a threat to performance, control, or even job security.

But here's the thing: lean doesn't mean lean people. It means lean waste. And the best way to combat resistance is to start by addressing the elephant in the room—change is hard. Acknowledge it openly, just as you would if a chef suddenly lost their go-to ingredient and had to rework their menu. Begin with empathy.

Lean initiatives that succeed often start informally—with grassroots ideas and small pilot projects rather than sweeping declarations. Think "lunch-and-learn" sessions where team members brainstorm improvements over pizza, or informal Gemba walks that invite front-line workers to point out inefficiencies in their own workflows. These moments build trust, foster ownership, and demonstrate that lean isn't about cutting jobs; it's about cutting frustration.

Encouraging dialogue is essential. Invite team members to share concerns, roadblocks, and creative ideas. Make it clear that lean isn't a top-down directive—it's a collaborative recipe. When people feel heard, they're more willing to try new techniques, just like a line cook might finally agree to prep vegetables with a mandoline after seeing how much faster and more consistent the results are.

Recognition also plays a powerful role. Highlight wins early and often—especially when a small change leads to a big result. Create a "lean leaderboard" or a "wall of improvement," and celebrate both individual and team contributions. Everyone loves to see their name on the menu, especially when it's tied to something meaningful.

In semiconductor environments, where processes are highly technical, even small adjustments—like reordering a tool setup or adjusting batch sizes—can significantly impact cycle time and yield. When teams see the real-time benefits of lean thinking, the resistance often melts away faster than butter in a hot pan.

Remember, people don't resist change—they resist being changed. So guide them like a head chef mentoring their crew: with patience, clear direction, and a belief in their potential. Because once the kitchen buys into the lean philosophy, that's when the real magic begins.

Lean Tools and Techniques - Mise en Place for the Modern Manufacturer

In every great kitchen, mise en place—everything in its place—is the sacred foundation of a smooth service. It's not just about neat stations or pre-chopped onions; it's about readiness, flow, and minimizing chaos. In the same way, lean tools and techniques are the mise en place of modern manufacturing—ensuring the right parts, processes, and people are positioned to deliver maximum efficiency with minimal waste.

Let's start with the basics: **5S**—Sort, Set in Order, Shine, Standardize, and Sustain. This isn't just housekeeping; it's culinary choreography. In semiconductor operations, where even a millimeter of misplaced equipment can impact cleanroom flow or delay high-precision processes, 5S helps maintain order. A well-organized tool crib, a properly labeled storage rack, or a clean production cell aren't aesthetic upgrades—they're performance enablers.

Next up: **Kaizen**, or continuous improvement. Think of it as a daily special—a small, iterative change that makes the operation tastier over time. Whether it's refining how wafers are transferred between tools, simplifying documentation, or shaving seconds off a setup process, Kaizen events empower front-line workers to find better ways. They're the equivalent of a chef constantly tasting and adjusting the seasoning mid-prep—never settling for "good enough."

Value Stream Mapping (VSM)is another powerful lean technique. It's like laying out the entire recipe—ingredients, prep time, cooking sequence, plating steps—and identifying where the bottlenecks and waste live. In semiconductor supply chains, where processes are complex and cross-functional, VSM helps visualize delays, redundant approvals, or excessive handoffs. Once visualized, inefficiencies become easier to eliminate—no more wondering why the soufflé keeps falling when the answer is baked into the prep timeline.

Then there's **Just-in-Time (JIT)** and **Kanban**, which help align inventory with real-time demand. JIT is like prepping only what's needed for that evening's service—no more, no less. In wafer fabs or module assembly lines, where shelf life and obsolescence are real risks, JIT and Kanban boards help keep the flow fresh, agile, and cost-effective.

Poka-yoke—mistake-proofing—is another unsung hero. In a kitchen, this might look like color-coded cutting boards for raw meat and vegetables. In manufacturing, it's sensors that prevent the wrong tool from operating or fixtures that ensure only one orientation of a part can be placed. It reduces rework and defects, especially in high-mix environments where human error can mean costly scrap or delays.

What ties all these tools together is mindset. Lean isn't just about technique—it's about thinking differently. It's about asking, "Why do we do it this way?" and being open to answers that may challenge decades of practice.

The truth is, great operations—like great meals—don't happen by accident. They're built from intention, insight, and a mise en place that empowers everyone in the kitchen to shine.

Case Study - When a Dash of Lean Changed the Whole Menu

Sometimes, all it takes is a pinch of the right method to transform an entire operation. That's the magic of lean—it doesn't just tweak processes; it can rewrite the whole recipe. Let's step into the kitchen of a real-world semiconductor operation where a dash of lean thinking didn't just save time—it saved millions and redefined the way the team cooked up results.

Enter a global chip assembly site in Southeast Asia—high-volume, high-variability, and battling a classic bottleneck: final test and inspection. Throughput was stalling, inventory was piling up like unbussed tables, and defect rates were quietly creeping upward. The leadership team was considering capital investment—another $5 million in automated test equipment—to increase capacity. But a savvy operations manager, with a background in lean, had another idea: "Let's walk the process."

What they found was startling. Technicians were spending up to 20% of their time on manual logging, equipment changeovers lacked standardization, and tools were often idle, waiting for batch completion. It wasn't that they needed more ovens; it was that their kitchen flow was off.

They started with a **Kaizen blitz**—a focused three-day improvement event. Cross-functional teams, from engineering to operators, were pulled into the room. Using **value stream mapping**, they pinpointed every wasted motion and non-value-added step. Standardized work instructions were rewritten. A simple **Kanban system** was implemented for test queue management. And most crucially, they introduced **visual controls** that showed everyone—from floor staff to supervisors—where parts were, what was ready, and what was stuck.

The results? Within six weeks, throughput increased by 28%. Defect rates dropped by 15%. Most importantly, the need for that $5 million capital investment? Gone. They had uncovered enough hidden capacity through lean that additional equipment was no longer necessary.

And it didn't stop there. Inspired by the outcome, the site launched a "Lean Menu Board" initiative—a running list of improvement ideas submitted by teams across shifts, from warehouse to engineering. What started as a cost-saving effort became a culture shift. The mindset changed from "firefighting" to "flavor refinement."

This case underscores what lean chefs know instinctively: you don't solve every problem with more ingredients. Sometimes, you solve it with sharper knives, better prep, and a tighter brigade.

Lean isn't about cutting corners—it's about cutting waste. When applied correctly, it doesn't just improve service—it changes the entire dining experience. Or, in this case, the entire fab.

Finishing with Finesse - Lean as a Way of Life

Lean isn't a diet—it's a lifestyle. And just like any great culinary philosophy, it's not about restriction but about refinement. It's the art of knowing which ingredients to spotlight, which steps to streamline, and how to deliver a dish—whether plated food or a final product—with precision, consistency, and flair.

For too long, "lean" was misunderstood as simply "less." Less inventory. Less time. Less labor. But in the hands of a skilled supply chain chef, lean is about more—more agility, more value, more quality, more satisfaction. It's the mise en place of manufacturing: everything in its place, every role defined, and every action deliberate.

From 5S to standard work, Kaizen to Kanban, we've seen how lean transforms chaos into choreography. We've watched floor teams go from frustrated to empowered. We've seen metrics shift from lagging to leading. And we've heard the hum of operations move from clunky and reactive to smooth and responsive.

But more than any tool or method, lean works best when it's infused into the kitchen culture. It's not just a project—it's a posture. A mindset. A shared belief that every process can be better, every team member has insight, and every problem is a chance to cook up a smarter solution.

And when resistance bubbles up—as it always does—we don't force compliance. We invite curiosity. We host lunch-and-learns like communal tastings. We reward the brave souls who try something new, who trim the fat, who find a better way to sauté the onions without burning the garlic. Because that's how lean becomes sticky. Not from top-down mandates, but from ground-up pride.

In the end, lean isn't about perfection. It's about pursuit. The daily discipline to ask: "What can we improve today? What's slowing us down, cluttering our space, or leaving a bad taste in our customers' mouths?"

As you wipe down the cutting board of this chapter, remember: lean is the heartbeat of a healthy operation. It keeps things flowing, keeps flavors balanced, and keeps your supply chain nimble, hungry, and ready for whatever's next.

So here's to simmering solutions that feed efficiency and flavor alike—"Bon appétit" to a kitchen that's lean, clean, and always cooking.

13

THE ART OF SOURCING – PROCUREMENT STRATEGIES

Sourcing as Strategy – Not Just Shopping with a Bigger Cart

IN THE SUPPLY CHAIN KITCHEN, sourcing is far more than a glorified grocery run. It's not just about finding the cheapest flour or the fastest delivery truck. It's about choosing the right farmers, understanding the seasons, cultivating trusted relationships, and knowing when to lock in a contract—or when to walk away. Sourcing is an art form, a dance between quality, cost, risk, and time. And when done right, it transforms procurement from a cost center into a competitive edge.

Think of it this way: a chef doesn't just grab the first tomatoes on the shelf—they know the supplier, the soil, and the climate that ripened the fruit. They source for flavor, not just price. Similarly, a skilled procurement professional sources for value—not just immediate savings, but long-term reliability, innovation potential, and ethical alignment.

In the semiconductor world, where a single faulty part can stall millions in revenue, sourcing is strategic survival. The lead times are long, the materials are rare, and the stakes are astronomical. From gallium arsenide to gold bonding wires, not all suppliers—or sourcing decisions—are created equal.

This chapter dives deep into how modern organizations elevate sourcing from transactional to transformative. We'll look at category strategies, supplier segmentation, risk-balanced portfolios, and the tools that empower teams to source smarter. We'll explore the flavor of global sourcing, the spice of local resilience, and the seasoning of sustainable procurement.

From negotiating like a seasoned sommelier to building supplier relationships that feel more like culinary collaborations than contracts, you'll learn how to approach procurement not as a back-office chore—but as a front-line strategy. Because in the end, great dishes start with great ingredients. And great supply chains? They start with sourcing that's intentional, informed, and infused with flavor.

So grab your market list, sharpen your instincts, and let's cook up a better way to procure.

Sourcing Smarter - From Commodity Buying to Strategic Procurement

Let's set the record straight: sourcing isn't just shopping with a badge. It's not about punching POs and chasing three quotes. Strategic procurement is the art of knowing which ingredients create the dish you want, sourcing them at the right time, and nurturing relationships that can weather the heat of any kitchen crisis. It's culinary precision fused with supply chain savvy—and when done right, it becomes the secret recipe behind every resilient operation.

In traditional commodity buying, the goal was simple: buy low, buy fast, move on. But in today's volatile and high-stakes environment—especially in the semiconductor world—this approach is about as useful as buying eggs from the cheapest vendor on the street corner during truffle season. Quality varies. Lead times slip. Risks multiply. And without a plan, the soufflé collapses.

Strategic procurement flips the script. It's less about chasing bargains and more about crafting a sourcing portfolio that supports business goals. Just like a chef curates local farms for peak-season produce and global imports for specialty ingredients, a strategic sourcing manager builds a balanced supplier base—local for speed, global for scale, and diverse for resilience.

Let's take capacitors as an example. Commodity buyers might chase the lowest unit cost, but a strategic sourcing team will consider lifecycle cost, inventory risk, geopolitical exposure, and quality history. They'll collaborate with engineering to understand technical specs, with finance to assess total landed cost, and with operations to plan buffers. It's like designing the pantry for the whole menu, not just one dish.

In high-tech manufacturing, this shift is critical. As product life cycles shrink and customer expectations rise, having the right supplier relationships isn't a luxury—it's a differentiator. Smart procurement organizations are embedding themselves upstream in product development, ensuring that what is sourced aligns with both innovation and scalability.

Take it from seasoned semiconductor players like Intel and Nvidia, who don't just source chips—they shape the ecosystem around them. They co-develop capabilities, invest in supplier tooling, and create joint roadmaps. That's not buying; that's strategic sourcing as a competitive weapon.

And the tools have evolved too. Spend analytics, supplier scorecards, risk dashboards, and digital procurement platforms provide visibility and foresight. It's no longer about gut feel—it's data, insight, and relationships working in concert. Like a chef adjusting seasoning by taste and technique, procurement leaders must blend instinct with intelligence.

In the end, sourcing smarter means thinking beyond today's order. It means designing a resilient supply base that delivers consistency, creativity, and competitive advantage. It's not just about filling the pantry; it's about curating the flavor profile of your entire operation.

Global Sourcing Challenges - From Exotic Ingredients to Complex Risks

In the culinary world, sourcing exotic ingredients can elevate a dish from familiar to unforgettable. But the rarer the spice, the more treacherous the journey from field to fork. In supply chain terms, global sourcing offers tantalizing rewards—cost advantages, innovation access, and scale—but it also stirs in a heady mix of complexity and risk. It's not unlike crafting a world tour on a single plate: brilliant if everything arrives on time, but a recipe for chaos if one link breaks.

In the semiconductor kitchen, global sourcing isn't optional—it's embedded into the DNA. Silicon wafers from Taiwan, packaging substrates from Japan, precious metals from South America, test sockets from Malaysia, and precision tooling from Germany—it's an intricate dance of interdependence. And with every added border comes new customs, compliance rules, and geopolitical baggage. When one partner sneezes, the entire supply chain catches a cold.

Take the 2021 fire at Renesas in Japan. It shut down a single chipmaking line—but sent ripple effects across the auto industry for months. Or the blockade in the Suez Canal. Or the China–U.S. trade tension over advanced lithography tools. Each of these was a single spark that ignited systemic disruption. This is what global sourcing in semiconductors looks like—high reward, high wire.

Then there are currency fluctuations, varying labor laws, and shipping constraints. Your sweet spot on the cost curve can suddenly turn sour when a trade tariff hits or a freight container gets stuck at sea. Global sourcing requires agility, not just appetite. You must know when to pivot suppliers, when to dual-source, and when to stockpile—even if your CFO grumbles about carrying costs.

Cultural and communication barriers also play a role. Misalignment over specs, unclear escalation paths, or differing quality expectations can lead to rework, missed deadlines, or worse—a failed product launch. That's why strategic sourcing isn't just about issuing POs; it's about building multilingual, cross-border relationships steeped in clarity, trust, and shared KPIs.

Technology can help—digital procurement tools provide transparency, scenario planning models stress-test vulnerabilities, and supplier portals offer real-time updates. But even with the best dashboards, global sourcing still requires human judgment, geopolitical foresight, and risk-balanced decision-making. It's both art and science, and like any ambitious fusion dish, it can delight or derail depending on the care taken in preparation.

So yes, sourcing globally means tapping into the world's pantry. But it also means being ready for everything from volcanic ash clouds to factory fires. The key is to treat complexity not as a flaw, but as a flavor—one that, when managed well, brings richness and resilience to your supply chain's table.

Supplier Relationship Management - Nurturing the Growers of Your Garden

In every great kitchen, there's an unspoken reverence for the growers—the farmers, foragers, fishmongers, and butchers who bring in the day's best ingredients. Without them, the chef is powerless. The same holds true in supply chains: suppliers aren't just vendors—they're the roots of your operation. Nurturing these relationships is like tending to your garden. Ignore it, and weeds grow. But cultivate it with intention, and it will feed your business for seasons to come.

Supplier Relationship Management (SRM) goes far beyond contract negotiations and quarterly business reviews. It's about investing in partnerships, co-creating value, and aligning incentives. In the high-stakes, high-spec world of semiconductors, this means working with your suppliers not just as transaction points, but as strategic collaborators—growers of innovation, not just inventory.

Strong SRM starts with segmentation. Not every supplier needs a seat at the chef's table, but your critical, high-impact partners? They need regular check-ins, shared roadmaps, and joint problem-solving sessions. This is where scorecards, capability audits, and shared KPIs come into play. Are they meeting your quality standards? Can they scale with your growth? Are they as committed to ESG, traceability, and cyber resilience as you are?

Great supplier relationships thrive on transparency. That means not just telling them what you need—but why. It means forecasting together, not in silos. Sharing insights, not just demands. For example, if a chip packaging partner in Singapore knows you're anticipating a surge in demand three quarters out, they can start investing in tooling or training ahead of time. You're not just placing orders—you're planting seeds.

It also means being there when the harvest is lean. Too often, companies squeeze suppliers during tough times, only to find themselves at the back of the line when the market recovers. Instead, be the partner who offers support—maybe extended payment terms during a crisis, maybe co-investment in capacity, or maybe just honest communication. Loyalty, like any crop, takes time and trust to grow.

And don't underestimate the human side of it. Celebrate wins together. Recognize innovation. Host supplier roundtables where ideas flow as freely as espresso at the end of a long service. These gestures, while soft in nature, build the type of rapport that turns transactional relationships into transformative ones.

At its best, SRM turns your supply chain into a community: a network of expert artisans and trusted allies who are just as invested in your success as you are. Because when you nurture your growers, they'll keep your pantry stocked—even when the weather turns.

Supplier Scorecards - Measuring What Matters on the Menu

In a five-star kitchen, you don't just guess if the fish is fresh or the sauce is seasoned—you measure, taste, and tweak. Likewise, in a world-class supply chain, supplier performance isn't left to gut feeling or anecdotal feedback. You need data. You need criteria. You need a scorecard—your mise en place for accountability.

A well-crafted supplier scorecard is more than a report card—it's your culinary critique sheet, measuring consistency, quality, responsiveness, and innovation. It helps you identify who's plating perfection every time and who might be cutting corners on prep. And just like in a kitchen, where performance reviews are immediate (no one forgets a burnt entrée), scorecards should offer regular, timely feedback—not just once a year when the soufflé is already sunk.

So, what should be on the menu? Start with the basics: **on-time delivery**, **order accuracy**, and **defect rates**. These are the salt, fat, and acid of your performance palate—essential indicators of operational health. But don't stop there. Great scorecards include **lead-time variability**, **cost competitiveness**, **sustainability practices**, **cybersecurity compliance**, and even **collaboration metrics**. After all, if your supplier is difficult to work with, that friction eventually shows up on the customer's plate.

For the semiconductor industry, the scorecard might also include **ECO (Engineering Change Order) responsiveness**, **cleanroom compliance**, and **capacity forecasting alignment**. These metrics reflect the complexity and precision demanded in chip production, where a single misstep in handling or a delay in response can derail a tightly orchestrated product launch.

But a scorecard is only as good as the conversation it sparks. That's why best-in-class organizations don't just send the scores—they host **supplier debriefs**, co-create **performance improvement plans**, and reward top performers. Some even showcase quarterly supplier awards, turning measurement into motivation. Think of it as plating up feedback with flair—constructive, not combative.

And let's not forget: scorecards should evolve. Just as a seasonal menu changes based on what's fresh and relevant, your KPIs should shift with strategic priorities. Is sustainability suddenly a top concern? Add emissions tracking or recycled material content. Are you expanding into new regions? Add regional compliance metrics or localization capabilities.

In the end, supplier scorecards help ensure you're sourcing from partners who share your standards—and your aspirations. They keep expectations clear, performance transparent, and partnerships grounded in shared growth. Because when everyone knows what's being measured, everyone plays to win. Or, in culinary terms, they know the difference between delivering a dish and delivering a masterpiece.

Sourcing Ethics - Keeping the Kitchen Clean

In every great kitchen, cleanliness isn't just a habit—it's a code. You wipe down your station, sanitize your tools, and ensure every ingredient meets your standards before it even hits the cutting board. Ethical sourcing in the supply chain world operates by the same principle. It's about more than compliance—it's about integrity, transparency, and ensuring that every link in your supply chain is as clean as your prep table before the dinner rush.

Sourcing ethics means asking hard questions: Where did this component come from? Were fair labor practices followed? Are we funding innovation—or exploitation? In the semiconductor world, where rare earth minerals and global labor markets intersect, these questions aren't hypothetical; they're urgent.

Take conflict minerals, for instance. Tantalum, tin, tungsten, and gold —essential for semiconductor production—are often mined in regions plagued by human rights abuses. Without due diligence, that silicon wafer in your fab could have a dark origin story. That's why frameworks like the **OECD Due Diligence Guidance** and the **Responsible Minerals Initiative (RMI)** exist: to keep your supply chain from becoming a crime scene.

But ethics goes beyond minerals. It includes **anti-bribery, intellectual property protection**, **environmental stewardship**, and **fair working conditions**. It's about making sure your suppliers aren't cutting corners or cutting wages. It's about ensuring their "kitchen" is free of forced labor, unsafe conditions, and practices that would leave any auditor—culinary or otherwise—gagging.

Semiconductor leaders are now embedding **ethics clauses** in supplier contracts, requiring **auditable codes of conduct**, and conducting **third-party social and environmental audits**. At companies like Intel, TSMC, and Apple, supplier ethics isn't a PR initiative—it's a business imperative. Clean hands lead to clean products, and clean products build trust with consumers, regulators, and investors alike.

Beyond compliance, ethics is about **values alignment**. Does your supplier support diversity? Are they minimizing emissions? Are they engaging their communities or merely extracting value from them? These aren't just nice-to-haves anymore—they're competitive differentiators. Customers and stakeholders want to know: what's the story behind the dish?

Like a restaurant that sources locally and lists its farms on the menu, supply chains can now showcase their ethical sourcing with transparency portals, sustainability dashboards, and real-time reporting. Ethics become part of the brand—proof that you're not just serving excellence but sourcing it responsibly.

So keep your kitchen clean. Scrub every link in the chain. Because in today's marketplace, sourcing ethics isn't a garnish—it's the main course.

Cost Structure Optimization - Trimming the Fat Without Losing Flavor

In any well-run kitchen, trimming fat isn't about cutting corners—it's about refining the dish. The same applies to supply chain cost structures. You're not hacking away at expenses just to save a few dollars. You're carving with precision, ensuring every slice enhances flavor, efficiency, and performance. Cost optimization isn't austerity—it's culinary finesse for your bottom line.

The challenge is real: in an inflationary world where labor costs are rising, materials are volatile, and transportation eats more margin than a hungry prep cook, procurement teams can't afford to just buy cheap—they need to buy smart. That means understanding every layer of your cost stack like a chef understands the layers of a perfect lasagna.

Start with **should-cost analysis**. Just as a chef knows the market price of seasonal tomatoes, strategic sourcing professionals need a deep understanding of what a product should cost based on materials, labor, overhead, and margin. It's not about being adversarial; it's about being informed. This arms you with facts when negotiating with suppliers and helps you sniff out when something is overpriced—or suspiciously underpriced.

Next comes **total cost of ownership (TCO)**—the full plate, not just the sticker price. That offshore vendor may offer a lower unit cost, but if the lead times are long, logistics are unreliable, or quality is inconsistent, you're paying the price elsewhere. TCO thinking factors in shipping, tariffs, defect rates, warehousing, returns, and service impact. It's about choosing ingredients that don't just look good on paper but perform flawlessly under pressure.

In the semiconductor world, **volume leverage**, **lifetime buys**, and **multi-year contracting** play a key role in cost control. It's like bulk-buying saffron when you know your signature paella isn't coming off the menu anytime soon. Meanwhile, **"design-to-cost" initiatives** ensure that procurement works hand in hand with engineering to select components that are not only high-performing but also cost-efficient from the very beginning.

Digital tools add an extra layer of seasoning. Advanced analytics, supplier cost modeling, and automated RFQ platforms strip inefficiencies from the buying process, flag opportunities, and enhance visibility into global cost trends. You can spot price creep, benchmark against peers, and identify where you're overpaying—just like a chef tracking food waste and reengineering the menu to stay profitable.

Ultimately, cost structure optimization is about balancing taste and expense. You don't want to serve a bland dish just because it's cheap—but you also can't pour truffle oil on everything and expect to stay in business. The art lies in discerning which ingredients are worth the splurge and which ones can be substituted without anyone noticing.

So sharpen your knives and your spreadsheets, because trimming the fat with skill ensures your supply chain stays lean, flavorful, and financially satisfying.

Case Study: When Procurement Became the Secret Ingredient

In every legendary kitchen, there's a moment when a dish goes from good to unforgettable—not because of what's on the surface, but because of one secret ingredient that ties it all together. In the world of supply chains, that unsung hero is often procurement. And when done right, it's not just about cost; it's about competitive advantage, resilience, and strategic foresight.

Take the case of a global chip assembly site in Texas that was struggling with painfully slow tool calibration turnaround. This delay was threatening production timelines and escalating costs. Traditional sourcing teams might have defaulted to big-name metrology vendors with a global reach. But a sharp-eyed procurement lead looked closer to home—and saw opportunity, not just a purchase.

They engaged a veteran-owned microenterprise located just a few miles from the fab. Initially scoped to provide only basic calibration support, the vendor quickly exceeded expectations. Within two quarters, turnaround times had improved by 25%. But the real twist? The vendor proactively developed a predictive maintenance app using off-the-shelf IoT sensors, allowing the site to flag issues before equipment failed. That wasn't in the original contract—but it became a recipe for shared success.

This wasn't just about finding a supplier. It was about cultivating a partner—someone who had both the technical chops and the agility to adapt. The procurement team didn't just buy a service; they built a solution. And in doing so, they sparked a wave of innovation that rippled across other manufacturing sites, transforming how calibration was viewed—from a cost center to a strategic differentiator.

Meanwhile, on the global stage, another sourcing team at a semiconductor packaging facility in Southeast Asia took a bold step toward should-cost transparency. Faced with volatile resin prices and a fragmented supplier base, they built detailed cost models and opened collaborative dialogues with key vendors. By aligning on data—not haggling over price—they unlocked long-term agreements with built-in cost indexing, shared rebates, and even co-funded sustainability initiatives.

The outcome? A 15% reduction in material spend, a more reliable supply, and a significantly smaller carbon footprint.

These stories underscore a powerful truth: **when procurement teams think beyond transactions and lean into strategy, they become catalysts for transformation**. They're no longer just keeping the pantry stocked; they're helping rewrite the recipe.

So whether it's finding hidden talent in your own backyard or using analytics to transform supplier relationships, procurement has the power to turn the ordinary into the extraordinary. The secret ingredient? A mindset shift—from buying to building, from cost-cutting to value creation.

14

SEASONING THE MIX - QUALITY CONTROL IN THE SUPPLY CHAIN

First Taste, Lasting Impression - Why Quality Control is the Final Garnish

IN ANY HIGH-END KITCHEN, you'll hear this often: "You eat with your eyes first." But what keeps diners coming back? That first bite—the temperature, the texture, the flavor balance. It's the final garnish that seals the experience. In the world of supply chain, **quality control** is that garnish—the assurance that every component, every process, and every finished product meets the expectations set at the very beginning.

You can have the most efficient sourcing team, the sleekest logistics network, and the most agile manufacturing setup—but if your product fails to meet spec, you're sending out a burnt soufflé with a silver spoon. And in the semiconductor industry, where nanometers matter and microscopic defects can compromise multi-million-dollar devices, there is zero room for sloppy plating.

Quality control (QC) is not just a checkbox at the end of production. It's a mindset—a discipline embedded throughout the supply chain like seasoning through every layer of a dish. It starts upstream, with the raw materials, and continues through every process step, from wafer fabrication to final test and packaging.

Modern QC systems are powered by a mix of sensory inspection (both man and machine), process monitoring, real-time analytics, and a strong feedback loop from customer returns or field failures. And just like a chef continuously tasting and adjusting, best-in-class supply chains monitor, refine, and validate—before defects leave the kitchen.

Consider a packaging line where minor contamination could impact chip yield. A smart QC system here uses **vision inspection, UV scans, and AI-enabled anomaly detection** to flag sub-millimeter issues invisible to the human eye. Not only does this prevent yield loss, but it enables traceability—down to the lot, machine, operator, and time of day. It's mise en place for the microchip.

But QC isn't only about machines. It's also about people. Just like in a kitchen, everyone needs to know the standard. The plating team can't compensate for an overcooked steak—and a shipping dock can't correct a poorly assembled board. That's why **building a quality culture** across teams is key—from supplier inspection audits to line-side QC training, and even empowering operators to pull the cord when something doesn't look right.

Ultimately, quality control is about trust. Trust that what you ship will perform. Trust that your processes are sound. And trust that your brand stands behind what it delivers. Because in the global supply chain, just like in fine dining, every customer bite begins with confidence in your craft.

Building a Recipe for Quality - Standards, Specs, and Systems That Work

Every great dish begins with a trusted recipe—precise, repeatable, and tested. It tells you exactly how much heat to apply, when to stir, and which ingredients to add and when. The same goes for quality control in the supply chain: **standards, specifications, and systems** are the recipe cards that keep everything consistent, delicious, and scalable.

Imagine running a Michelin-starred kitchen without recipes—chaotic, right? One line cook adds too much salt, another undercooks the duck, and suddenly your signature dish is a shadow of itself. In semiconductor manufacturing, that's the equivalent of a fab operating without clearly defined process control limits or a supplier shipping parts based on assumptions rather than exacting prints. The margin for error disappears when you're working in nanometers, and so does your customer's patience.

Quality standards—like ISO 9001, IATF 16949, or IPC-A-610 for electronic assemblies—provide the structured foundation, ensuring every facility and supplier adheres to global benchmarks. These aren't just paperwork; they're the mise en place of operational excellence. They ensure that every process step, inspection point, and product characteristic has been thought through and aligned to expectations.

But standards alone aren't enough. You need **specifications**—the detailed technical "flavor profile" of your product. In the semiconductor world, that means thickness tolerances on wafers, electrical continuity on PCBs, flatness criteria on ceramic lids, and ESD-safe packaging. Specs define what's acceptable, what's ideal, and what's absolutely not allowed. They prevent ambiguity, and they protect relationships—because when everyone agrees on what the perfect dish looks like, it's easier to know when something's off.

Layered on top of these are **systems**—digital and procedural frameworks that ensure quality isn't dependent on memory or mood. Think "Statistical Process Control (SPC) charts," "Manufacturing Execution Systems (MES)," "Advanced Product Quality Planning (APQP)," and "Failure Mode and Effects Analysis (FMEA)." These tools serve as the sous-chefs of quality—watching every step, alerting the team when the mix goes off course, and keeping the operation in sync.

And like any good recipe, these systems evolve. Feedback loops from customer complaints, RMA analysis, in-line test data, and supplier scorecards are all ingredients for refinement. Continuous improvement isn't just a slogan—it's the act of tasting the sauce every day and adding just the right pinch of salt to keep it perfect.

In short, when standards, specs, and systems work together, quality becomes instinctual—not just enforced. It's like muscle memory for the supply chain: each batch, each lot, each unit plated with precision, every single time.

Inspection and Testing - Catching the Undercooked and Overdone

In any professional kitchen, no dish leaves the pass without a final inspection. The chef takes one last look—does the sauce have the right sheen? Are the garnishes aligned just so? Is the steak medium rare, not medium well? It's that moment of truth where quality is either confirmed or corrected. In the world of supply chains—especially in semiconductor operations—**inspection and testing** serve exactly that purpose. They are the final tasting spoon before your product hits the customer's plate.

Just as you wouldn't serve a soufflé without checking if it's risen, you wouldn't ship a microchip without ensuring its functionality. Inspection and testing are the **gatekeepers of quality**, catching the defects that specs and systems might have missed. And in a world of microscopic tolerances and invisible errors, these processes must be as precise as a surgeon's scalpel—and just as non-negotiable.

Incoming inspections are the first line of defense, much like a chef examining produce deliveries before accepting the goods. Is the copper plating uniform? Are dimensions within spec? Are the parts ESD-compliant and uncontaminated? Skipping this step is like blindly throwing ingredients into the pot—you risk ruining the entire dish before you've even begun cooking.

Once materials pass the door, **in-process inspections** and **real-time testing** ensure that every phase of production follows the recipe. In the semiconductor industry, this might mean electrical tests on wafers, automated optical inspection (AOI) for PCB assemblies, or surface particle detection in cleanrooms. These aren't just quality checks—they're risk containment points, preventing defects from snowballing further down the line.

Then there's **final inspection**—your equivalent of the head chef wiping the plate and adjusting the garnish before service. Whether it's a functional test for performance, burn-in testing for reliability, or visual checks for cosmetic flaws, this step ensures that only the best makes it out the door.

Modern quality kitchens also employ **statistical sampling, AQL thresholds**, and **automated test equipment (ATE)** that reduce subjectivity and boost efficiency. And when you're dealing with thousands—or millions—of units, you need systems that can do more than just inspect. You need systems that **learn**. That's where machine vision, AI-driven defect classification, and traceability solutions turn inspection into insight. Suddenly, you're not just spotting flaws—you're identifying trends, root causes, and future risks.

Ultimately, inspection and testing are not about catching blame—they're about **catching opportunities**. The opportunity to protect your brand. To exceed customer expectations. To serve a consistently excellent experience. Because in supply chain, as in fine dining, it's not just about getting the order out—it's about making sure every bite (or byte) is worth remembering.

Continuous Improvement - Refining the Recipe Over Time

In the best kitchens, the recipe is never truly finished. Even after the dish is on the menu and drawing five-star reviews, the chef keeps tweaking—adding a pinch more acidity here, shaving seconds off the cook time there. Why? Because true excellence isn't a destination; it's a process. And that philosophy lies at the heart of **continuous improvement** in supply chain quality control.

In semiconductor operations, where defect tolerance is measured in parts per billion, the pursuit of perfection isn't just aspirational—it's operational. Continuous improvement ensures that every step of the process, from raw material sourcing to final packaging, becomes progressively better, smarter, and more resilient. It's how good supply chains become great—and how great ones stay on top.

The framework for this philosophy often starts with **Kaizen**—the Japanese term for "change for the better." This mindset encourages every team member, from line operators to supply managers, to be chefs in their own right—observing, questioning, adjusting, and innovating at every opportunity. It's about empowering the kitchen crew to refine the prep list, not just to follow it.

In practice, continuous improvement might look like conducting **Root Cause Analysis (RCA)** on recurring quality failures, deploying **Corrective and Preventive Actions (CAPAs)**, or running **Design of Experiments (DOE)** to tweak process parameters for optimal outcomes. In a packaging fab, it might mean adjusting plasma etch parameters based on yield data; in a board assembly line, it could involve refining soldering profiles to reduce joint defects. Every refinement is a step toward a recipe that's not just repeatable, but exceptional.

Quality circles and **cross-functional Kaizen events** bring diverse minds together—engineering, operations, procurement, and quality control—each contributing a different palate to refine the process. These collaborative efforts often uncover blind spots or systemic flaws that solo chefs might miss.

Technology plays its role here, too. Advanced analytics, real-time dashboards, and machine learning models can help identify subtle trends in quality data that humans might overlook. Imagine a system that flags a pattern in micro-cracks on silicon wafers that occur only under specific humidity conditions—then suggests preventive measures. That's not just quality control; it's culinary intuition powered by AI.

But continuous improvement isn't just about reacting to issues—it's about proactively elevating performance. It's about celebrating small wins, learning from every misstep, and keeping the curiosity alive.

Because even when the dish is good enough, the great chef asks, "Could it be even better?"

In the end, refining the recipe over time keeps your supply chain dynamic, responsive, and ever-evolving. It transforms quality control from a checklist into a craft—and your operation from a static kitchen into a living laboratory of excellence.

Case Study - When Quality Saved the Dish

Sometimes, it's not the new product launch or the shiny innovation that earns the standing ovation—it's the quiet, consistent commitment to quality that saves the day. Enter this real-world tale from the semiconductor world: a global chipmaker was preparing for a critical product release that hinged on a new advanced node process. The customer? A top-tier smartphone OEM with zero tolerance for delays. The pressure? Like plating the final course for a panel of Michelin inspectors.

Midway through the ramp-up, yield rates on a key wafer process began to mysteriously decline. Not drastically—but just enough to raise red flags. Some leaders considered pushing forward, but the quality team insisted on pausing. Their instincts said the dish wasn't ready. And that pause? It turned out to be the most important decision in the entire rollout.

The investigation led to a seemingly minor equipment calibration drift in a plasma etching tool—off by less than 0.3%, barely noticeable. But in a world where nanometers matter, that tiny variation was causing micro-defects that would have led to latent product failures once chips hit the field. Without a robust inspection process and a culture that respected quality escalation, the issue might have gone undetected until customers experienced it—costing millions in recalls, damaging brand trust, and delaying future product launches.

Instead, the fab's commitment to continuous improvement kicked in. A cross-functional team ran a root cause analysis, isolated the fault, recalibrated all similar tools, and implemented real-time monitoring thresholds to prevent recurrence. The entire incident was resolved within a week—with no impact on the product launch timeline. The dish had nearly burned, but a well-trained kitchen caught it in time and saved the service.

The client never saw the smoke in the kitchen. All they saw was a flawless product delivered on time and a partner they could trust to deliver again and again. That's the power of quality control—not just in preventing defects, but in protecting relationships, brand equity, and long-term value.

In the culinary world, great chefs don't just cook to order—they prepare with discipline, recover from missteps, and elevate the dish every time it is served. In supply chain, the same applies: quality isn't a checkpoint—it's the signature seasoning that elevates everything it touches.

15

COOKING UNDER PRESSURE – HANDLING CRISES

When the Kitchen Catches Fire – The Nature of Crisis in Supply Chains

IN EVERY CHEF'S CAREER, there comes a moment when the heat gets too high, the orders pile up, and the power flickers just as the soufflés are rising. In supply chains, those moments are called crises. Whether it's a factory fire, a geopolitical shutdown, a cyberattack, or a global pandemic—crises don't just test your operations; they test your preparation, leadership, and grit.

Crises are the kitchen infernos of the corporate world. They don't knock—they burst through the door mid-service. And like any seasoned chef will tell you, how you respond when everything is burning is what separates the cooks from the culinary legends.

Semiconductor supply chains are especially vulnerable to these flashpoints. The level of complexity, capital intensity, and reliance on long lead-time components means there's little room for improvisation. A two-week disruption in raw materials can cascade into months of missed output—like a missing ingredient delaying every dish on the menu.

Just as a top kitchen drills for fire drills and power outages, a world-class supply chain must embed crisis playbooks directly into its DNA. This isn't about waiting for disaster to strike; it's about designing a kitchen that can keep cooking even when the lights go out.

At the heart of effective crisis management is **resilience through preparation**. That means knowing your critical paths, your single points of failure, and your "must-serve" orders. It means cross-training your staff, keeping your tools sharp, and having a backup station that can be fired up at a moment's notice.

It's also about **leadership under pressure**—how you communicate, how fast you mobilize, and how clearly you can prioritize. The best crisis leaders aren't the loudest in the room—they're the ones who know which pot to pull off the stove first and which one can simmer just a bit longer.

And finally, there's the **post-crisis mise en place**—the reflection, the learning, the systems improvement. Every crisis, no matter how chaotic, is a teacher in disguise. The scars it leaves behind can become the muscle memory that sharpens your next response.

In this chapter, we'll explore how to build a crisis-ready operation—one that can withstand the burn, adapt on the fly, and come out the other side stronger. From crisis identification and playbook development to rapid communication and case studies from the front lines, we're going to show you how to stay calm when the kitchen goes full tilt.

Because in this business, **cooking under pressure** isn't a risk—it's a requirement. And if you've prepped right, even the worst nights can still end in applause.

Recognizing the Boil - How to Spot a Crisis Before It Erupts

In every great kitchen, a seasoned chef knows how to spot trouble before it bubbles over. A sauce that's reducing too fast, a burner that's flaring too hot, or a sous-chef who suddenly looks pale under pressure

—these early signs are the difference between salvaging a dish and sending smoke signals to the fire marshal. The same principle holds true in supply chain crisis management. The ability to recognize the early boil—those subtle signals of stress and strain—can mean the difference between agile intervention and catastrophic fallout.

Crises rarely arrive unannounced. They start with tremors: a slight uptick in supplier lead times, a pattern of missed deliveries, or unexplained scrap rate increases. In semiconductor supply chains, where every part and process is tightly interwoven, even a minor fluctuation—like a temperature deviation in cleanroom equipment or a delay in packaging substrates—can cascade quickly. The trick is learning to spot the signs before the rolling boil.

This requires both human intuition and technological support. On the floor, team members who are close to the process often notice things before dashboards do: a vendor's tone shifting in meetings, repeated quality exceptions swept under the rug, or a key supplier's hiring freeze. These are your "canaries in the coal mine" signals that something is off-kilter.

At the same time, digital systems must be tuned for early warning. Predictive analytics tools can flag trends long before they become problems. Maybe there's a regional uptick in political instability. Maybe ocean freight reliability is slipping below 40% for a specific port. Or maybe there's a spike in demand that your reorder point hasn't yet reflected. These signals are like steam rising from the pot—if you wait until the boil, it might already be too late.

Establishing clear escalation protocols is also essential. A delay should never come as a surprise. If the team knows exactly what metrics trigger an internal alert—or, better yet, if those alerts are automated—you'll have time to adjust your recipe before it burns. This could mean rerouting shipments, activating backup suppliers, or accelerating production on an alternate line.

Finally, culture plays a big role. Create an environment where people aren't afraid to call out the early signs—even if they turn out to be false alarms. Just like in a kitchen, you'd rather have someone shout "Smoke!" over a caramelizing sauce than stay silent and let it catch fire.

The best crisis managers don't just react—they read the room. They know that every boil begins with a simmer. And in a world where every second counts, that early detection might be the most valuable tool in your apron pocket.

Stirring the Pot - Leading Through the Boil, Not Just the Simmer

In a bustling kitchen, the difference between a memorable service and a full-blown meltdown often lies in leadership. When the grill flames too high, when the walk-in fridge goes down mid-rush, or when a VIP table demands a custom dish in five minutes, the best chefs don't panic—they pivot. They take charge, stir the pot, and get the crew focused. In a supply chain crisis, especially in high-stakes industries like semiconductors, that same cool-headed, hands-on leadership is what turns chaos into control.

The truth is, when a crisis hits, all eyes turn to the leader. And it's not just about having the answers—it's about setting the tone. Do you bring clarity or confusion? Direction or drama? A true supply chain leader becomes the executive chef of the moment—coordinating the brigade, calming the chaos, and keeping communication crisp and clear.

Let's take an example from the semiconductor world: when COVID-19 hit and borders began closing, a packaging facility in the Philippines faced an immediate labor shortage. One shift went down, then two. Instead of sending reactive emails or waiting for corporate directives, the local leadership team activated its crisis playbook, repurposed idle cleanroom staff to help with non-critical packaging lines, and began daily stand-ups with procurement, logistics, and customers. The result? While output dipped, they maintained customer confidence and recovered faster than neighboring sites.

Leading through the boil means making fast but thoughtful decisions. It's triage: What must be fixed now? What can wait? What risks must be accepted? A good leader knows how to "thin the sauce"—removing nonessentials and focusing on the base. In supply chain terms, that might mean pausing lower-priority production, reallocating labor, or negotiating partial deliveries with key customers.

Transparency is your stock base—it keeps everything else flavorful. In a crisis, stakeholders crave communication. Whether it's your suppliers, customers, or executive team, silence breeds speculation. Just as a chef calls out order updates across the line, a supply chain leader should be over-communicating: status updates, risk scenarios, and mitigation plans. People want to know someone is at the pass, keeping track of the orders.

And don't forget your team. High-pressure moments test morale, endurance, and unity. Recognize the grind. Celebrate the micro-wins. And above all, stay present. The best leaders aren't watching the fire from the office—they're on the line, tasting, adjusting, and reminding everyone that the kitchen still runs on passion and purpose.

Because when the pot is boiling, what your team needs most isn't perfection—it's presence, decisiveness, and a steady hand on the ladle.

The Pressure Cooker Plan - Developing a Crisis Management Recipe

A crisis isn't the time to start planning—it's the moment when you test the recipe you've already written. Just like a pressure cooker demands careful preparation, so does your supply chain when the heat is on. You don't want to be dicing vegetables while the pot is already whistling. You need a plan—a recipe for resilience—that outlines what to do when your normal processes are upended by the unexpected.

Developing a crisis management plan starts with anticipating the types of crises most likely to bubble up in your operation. Natural disasters? Political unrest? Supplier insolvency? Cyberattacks? Think of each as a different high-risk ingredient. You wouldn't store shellfish the same way you store flour—and you shouldn't prepare for a port strike the same way you would for a power outage in your primary fab.

Begin with a risk matrix that scores both likelihood and impact—your mise en place for disruption. Rank your risks. Define your thresholds. Determine your critical path processes and suppliers. Just like a pastry chef sets timers down to the second, you need clear escalation triggers: what specific events or signals should immediately set the plan in motion?

Then, codify roles and responsibilities. Who is your crisis lead? Who's on comms? Who owns supplier engagement, customer updates, logistics rerouting, and financial impact modeling? Like a brigade kitchen, everyone must know their station—and their backup, too.

Next, develop scenario playbooks. Each one should include immediate response actions (first 24–48 hours), stabilization steps (within a week), and recovery objectives (1–3 months out). For example, one OSAT facility built a playbook for a potential power grid failure, pre-negotiated fuel contracts for backup generators, tested the shift-to-night operations plan, and established a customer notification protocol. When the blackout did come, they didn't scramble—they served.

But planning isn't enough. You need to train. Simulate. Run drills. A crisis plan that lives in a drawer might as well be a soufflé recipe no one's tested. Conduct tabletop exercises. Walk through what happens if your top supplier in Malaysia goes offline, or if your ocean freight is held up in customs due to a regulatory change. The more you rehearse, the more intuitive your response becomes.

Finally, build in a feedback loop. After every real-world or simulated event, conduct a post-mortem: What went well, what went wrong, and what needs to change? Crisis readiness, like any great recipe, improves with refinement.

The goal isn't to eliminate the pressure—it's to cook with it. A well-prepared crisis plan ensures that even when your kitchen hits the boiling point, you can still plate excellence with calm, confidence, and control.

Recovering After the Burn - Rebuilding with Strength

Every kitchen has its disasters—burnt sauces, collapsed cakes, the occasional fire drill that clears the entire floor. But what separates the amateur from the master chef is not whether something goes wrong, but how they rebuild after the burn. In the world of supply chains, recovery is just as critical as response. Because once the smoke clears, it's not about returning to normal—it's about coming back stronger, smarter, and more resilient than before.

Recovery begins by owning the mess. Transparency matters. Whether it's a missed shipment or a week-long production delay, communicate clearly with stakeholders: what happened, what's being done, and what's next. Customers can forgive disruption—what they don't forgive is silence or spin. The same goes internally. Leadership must create a blame-free zone that encourages honest post-mortems and root-cause analysis. This is where lessons are seared into institutional memory.

Let's say your lead wafer supplier in South Korea experienced a two-week shutdown due to flooding. The initial crisis response stabilized the situation. But what now? Recovery isn't just about plugging the gap; it's about rethinking the structure: Should we dual-source? Should we shift volume to a fab in Singapore? Do we need a strategic stockpile or a different buffer strategy? Treat the crisis as your chance to redesign the recipe.

One analog company took that very approach. After a cyberattack disrupted production for 10 days, they used the downtime to accelerate cloud migration, decentralize data access, and implement multi-tiered backups that hadn't been prioritized before. The result wasn't just restored service; it was a fortified digital kitchen capable of withstanding future heat.

This stage of the process should also include supplier engagement. Don't just dust off the apron and move on—reconnect with your partners. Understand how the crisis impacted them. Co-develop new guardrails. Review SLAs, diversify transportation lanes, invest in visibility tools, or even collaborate on shared inventory models. Your recovery plan shouldn't be a solo dish—it's a potluck of collective resilience.

Finally, celebrate the wins—however small. Did the team rally and pivot in record time? Did a junior planner flag a crucial risk? Recognition fuels morale, and morale fuels retention. A crisis might scald the surface, but it can also forge deeper team cohesion and sharpen strategic thinking.

Because rebuilding isn't just about patching holes. It's a creative act. It's mise en place for the future, rebuilt on stronger ground, seasoned by experience, and plated with purpose. And when the next wave of pressure arrives—as it inevitably will—you'll be ready to respond not just with instinct but with insight.

Case Studies: Crises That Changed the Menu

Every seasoned chef knows that a burnt dish can sometimes inspire a new signature plate. In the same way, some of the most disruptive supply chain crises have yielded unexpected innovations, forged stronger partnerships, and sparked permanent changes in strategy. Let's step into the kitchens of a few real-world companies that turned up the heat—and came out with new recipes for success.

Case 1: The Chip Shortage Heard 'Round the World – Auto Industry Rethinks Its Pantry

The COVID-19 pandemic triggered one of the most widely publicized supply chain disruptions in modern history: the global semiconductor shortage. Auto manufacturers, who had long relied on just-in-time inventory models, found themselves scrambling for microchips that were suddenly nowhere to be found. Factories halted production. Revenue tanked. Executives panicked.

But from that crisis came a strategic menu overhaul. Ford and GM began forging direct relationships with chipmakers—something they had previously left to Tier 1 suppliers. Toyota increased its semiconductor buffer stock by up to six months. Others invested in joint ventures with fabless chip designers. The industry realized that chips weren't a garnish—they were the main protein. And they needed to be treated as such in every sourcing strategy moving forward.

Case 2: The Sriracha Shortage – When Climate Turned Up the Heat

When Huy Fong Foods—the maker of the cult-favorite Sriracha sauce—faced a chili pepper shortage due to drought conditions in Mexico, fans around the world were left with empty shelves. The supplier's sole pepper source had become a single point of failure.

In response, Huy Fong began reevaluating its sourcing and farming strategies. Although not a semiconductor company, the lesson holds: no matter how good the ingredient, relying on one exclusive farm (or supplier) is a high-stakes gamble. Semiconductor firms took note, with some diversifying their own supplier bases and investing in vertical farming technologies to secure plant-based materials for green packaging.

Case 3: Flooding in Thailand – A Wake-Up Call for Storage Strategy

In 2011, record-breaking floods in Thailand submerged industrial parks and took out nearly half of the world's hard disk drive (HDD) production. The disaster not only halted manufacturing but also revealed how much capacity was concentrated in a single region.

Major tech companies like Western Digital and Seagate responded by redesigning their global footprint. They spread out production across multiple geographies, diversified logistics channels, and invested in flood-resistant infrastructure. Some shifted product focus toward solid-state drives (SSDs) to reduce regional dependency. The incident reinforced the value of geographic diversity—not just for natural disaster mitigation but also for long-term strategic flexibility.

Culinary Takeaway

Each of these stories underscores a universal truth: crises are inevitable, but catastrophe is optional. The menu may change, but the kitchen keeps running—smarter, faster, and more collaboratively. When organizations stop viewing crises as temporary setbacks and start treating them as catalysts for reinvention, they build the kind of muscle memory that can weather any storm.

Because sometimes, when the sauce breaks or the oven fails, the best chefs don't just recover—they innovate. They create a new dish altogether.

Turning the Heat into Mastery - A Final Reduction

In every great kitchen, pressure isn't just a threat—it's a tool. It's the hiss of the pressure cooker, the sizzle of a hot pan, the pulse of adrenaline before the first plate hits the pass. And in supply chain management, crisis works the same way. When handled with poise, clarity, and grit, it doesn't just reveal weakness—it builds strength. Like a tough cut of meat transformed by a slow braise, organizations that lean into crisis come out more tender, more flavorful, and far more resilient.

From global chip shortages to climate-induced raw material disruptions, the last decade has been a pressure test for supply chains everywhere. And yet, those that survived—and thrived—didn't do so by luck. They did it through preparation, clear communication, scenario planning, and the courage to throw out the old recipe when it stopped serving the table.

Crises force us to ask the tough questions: Who are our most reliable partners? How quickly can we pivot? Are our teams aligned under stress, or scrambling in the dark? The answers don't just shape the response—they shape the future.

Because let's face it—disruption is the new constant. But so is opportunity. Every fire drill teaches us where the real exits are. Every "burnt dish" shows us how we could have plated smarter. And every recovery—no matter how hard-fought—builds a foundation for something stronger, faster, and more flavorful.

So, the next time the heat rises, don't reach for the fire extinguisher first. Reach for your team. Review your mise en place. Rely on your training, your data, and your instincts. Remember that great kitchens don't just survive chaos—they transform it.

Because, in the end, pressure doesn't ruin the recipe—it refines the chef.

16

SUSTAINABLE FLAVORS - ECO-FRIENDLY PRACTICES IN THE SUPPLY CHAIN

The Green Kitchen - Building Sustainability from Prep to Plate

A GREAT DISH doesn't just taste good—it feels good. And increasingly, the same goes for the supply chains that serve the global table. In a world where consumers demand transparency, regulators require accountability, and investors reward environmental stewardship, sustainability isn't a garnish. It's a core ingredient. It's the difference between a meal that nourishes and one that leaves a bad taste. And just like in a top-tier kitchen, every action—from sourcing ingredients to how we wash the pans—matters.

In the semiconductor industry, where high energy use, water consumption, and rare earth material sourcing pose significant environmental challenges, sustainability has become a boardroom-level priority. Factories guzzle gigawatts. Fab processes require ultrapure water by the millions of gallons. And the sourcing of certain metals—cobalt, tantalum, and gold—can trace roots to regions of conflict or fragile ecosystems. Without deliberate strategy, even the most efficient supply chain can leave behind a heavy carbon footprint.

So how do we shift from "greasy spoon" to "green cuisine"?

It starts at the ingredient level—raw materials and suppliers. Forward-thinking companies are partnering with vendors who share their commitment to sustainability. This might include requiring ISO 14001 certifications, mandating transparent sourcing practices, or collaborating on reducing packaging waste. One OSAT partner in Malaysia now packages chip trays in compostable material made from palm fiber waste—a beautiful example of turning kitchen scraps into supply chain value.

Then there's the matter of energy use. Just as a restaurant might switch to induction stoves or solar panels, semiconductor firms are investing in clean power and more efficient facilities. TSMC, for instance, has committed to sourcing 100% renewable energy for all global operations by 2050—a tall order, but one that is being steadily baked into procurement contracts, facility design, and even chip architecture.

Water is another vital "ingredient." Like a chef who filters and reuses water for blanching, fabs are increasingly installing closed-loop water systems, reducing discharge and treating wastewater to meet strict environmental standards. Intel's campuses in the U.S., for example, now return more water to the local watershed than they draw—a benchmark of how sustainability can align with operational excellence.

But let's not forget the "prep" behind the scenes—logistics, packaging, and warehousing. Green logistics means rerouting for efficiency, consolidating shipments, and investing in electric fleets or intermodal transport. Warehouses are being retrofitted with smart lighting, climate sensors, and automation that reduces waste—not unlike a kitchen that trains its staff to portion properly and store ingredients with care.

Sustainability is not about perfection. It's about intention. It's about building systems that reduce harm, foster innovation, and leave a lighter footprint without sacrificing flavor—or performance. When your supply chain is designed with the planet in mind, you're not just future-proofing your business; you're serving something better—something the world is hungry for.

So sharpen your green knives. We're not just feeding the bottom line anymore; we're feeding the future.

Sourcing Responsibly - Ethical Ingredients and Transparent Origins

Every chef worth their salt knows that the quality of the dish starts with the quality of the ingredients. But it's no longer just about taste or texture—it's about story. Where did the cacao come from? Who grew the saffron? Was the seafood ethically caught, or are you serving up a side of exploitation with that scallop? In supply chain terms, sourcing responsibly means peeling back the layers of the origin story and ensuring every supplier, miner, farmer, and factory worker in your extended ecosystem is treated with fairness, respect, and dignity.

This is especially critical in industries like semiconductors, where the trail from raw material to finished product spans continents and dozens of touchpoints. Materials like tantalum, tungsten, tin, and gold —known as "3TG"—are vital to chipmaking, yet often originate in regions prone to conflict or labor abuse. Ignoring that reality is no longer an option. The modern supply chain must act like a conscientious chef—reading the labels, vetting the vendors, and refusing to work with suppliers whose values don't align with ethical sourcing.

Frameworks like the Responsible Business Alliance (RBA) and OECD Due Diligence Guidance for Responsible Supply Chains aren't just bureaucratic checkboxes. They're the ethical mise en place that ensures human rights, anti-corruption practices, and environmental standards are baked into every contract. More and more, companies are requiring suppliers to submit Conflict Minerals Reporting Templates (CMRTs), undergo audits, and implement grievance mechanisms. It's like conducting surprise kitchen inspections to ensure every dish served is up to standard—not just in flavor, but in ethics.

Transparency is the hero of this story. Blockchain and digital traceability tools are emerging as powerful sous-chefs, offering real-time lineage tracking from mine to motherboard. Imagine being able to scan a component and see its full journey—from a certified conflict-free smelter in Rwanda to an IC packaging house in Penang. That's not science fiction; it's the new standard. The more transparent your ingredients, the more trustworthy your menu.

And let's not underestimate the brand advantage. Consumers, especially in tech, are smarter and more values-driven than ever. They want to know if their gadgets were built with exploitation or empowerment. Investors are also sharpening their focus, tying ESG scores to access to capital and shareholder value. What once lived in the CSR report now lives in the P&L.

Responsible sourcing isn't a constraint; it's a compass. It tells you where your values lie and guides your partnerships toward greater integrity, sustainability, and resilience. When you know exactly what's in your pantry—and how it got there—you're not just managing risk; you're serving a story that your customers and stakeholders will proudly consume.

Waste Not, Want Not - Designing Out Waste Across the Chain

In the kitchen, waste is the silent profit killer. That bruised tomato, that over-portioned plate, that sauce left congealing in the corner—all of it adds up, not just in cost but in conscience. The same goes for supply chains. Every pallet of obsolete components, every unused die, and every over-engineered part gathering dust in a warehouse is a missed opportunity for efficiency, sustainability, and savings.

Designing out waste isn't about cutting corners—it's about sharpening the knife. It means thinking upstream and engineering processes that eliminate excess before it even exists. In supply chain terms, this starts with **design for sustainability (DfS)**. Just like a chef plans their menu around seasonal, local produce to minimize spoilage, companies must design products with end-of-life, recyclability, and minimal material use in mind. In semiconductors, this could mean consolidating component counts, reducing packaging layers, or shifting to modular product designs that extend lifecycle and enable reuse.

Inventory waste is another critical offender. Overproduction, safety stock hoarding, and misaligned forecasts result in what the industry lovingly calls "dead inventory"—but really, it's just landfill in waiting. Lean inventory practices, such as **just-in-time** (JIT) replenishment, **pull systems**, and **Kanban signals**, can help kitchens and fabs alike align material flow with real demand. One Southeast Asia-based OSAT partner reengineered its inbound logistics with demand-triggered kitting. The result? A 28% reduction in material overstock and fewer scrapped assemblies due to shelf-life expiration.

Waste also hides in energy and motion: lights left on in an empty cleanroom, equipment idling between builds, and excessive handling steps that mirror a kitchen crew running laps between the stove and fridge. Enter **green lean** practices—process audits that pinpoint energy leaks, excess handling, and inefficiencies. A fab in Europe reduced its annual electricity bill by €2.3 million simply by optimizing airflow and load-balancing its HVAC system. Not glamorous, but game-changing.

Packaging waste deserves its own chapter. In a world still addicted to plastic foam and single-use anti-static wraps, forward-thinking supply chains are shifting to **returnable, reusable, and recyclable** packaging. Foam-free wafer cassettes, molded pulp trays, and RFID-enabled totes are replacing traditional throwaways. These changes may seem small, but they create massive reductions in carbon footprint and disposal costs.

Ultimately, designing out waste is about honoring the full lifecycle of every resource. It's a mindset—like a zero-waste chef who uses every part of the vegetable, turns scraps into stock, and composts the rest. When supply chains adopt this same reverence, they become not just leaner but greener, more ethical, and more future-proof.

Carbon-Conscious Cooking – Measuring and Managing Emissions

Every chef knows that a smoky kitchen isn't just a fire hazard—it's a sign that something's gone wrong. In the same way, a supply chain spewing unchecked emissions is a red flag, not just for the planet but for the business. In today's carbon-conscious marketplace, measuring and managing your emissions isn't a side dish—it's the main course.

It's what separates a sustainable operation from one that's being left to burn.

To start, supply chain emissions are typically divided into three "scopes," like layers in a lasagna:

Scope 1 covers direct emissions—think of gas burned by your own facilities or vehicles.

Scope 2 involves indirect emissions from the energy you purchase, like electricity to power your cleanrooms or warehouses.

Scope 3 is the big enchilada: all the emissions up and down your supply chain, from raw material extraction to product use and disposal.

Scope 3 often accounts for over 70% of a semiconductor company's carbon footprint, and it's notoriously hard to track. But just like a meticulous chef logs every gram of truffle, modern companies are investing in tools to measure even the most elusive carbon contributions. Carbon accounting platforms, lifecycle assessment software, and supplier emission calculators are becoming essential kitchenware in this sustainability toolkit.

The key is visibility. You can't reduce what you don't measure. That's why industry leaders like Intel and Micron are working directly with Tier 1 and Tier 2 suppliers to capture emissions data across manufacturing processes, transportation modes, and packaging choices. These collaborative initiatives help build a transparent carbon trail—from silicon ingot to end-user device.

Take logistics, for example. Shifting from air freight to ocean may take more time, but it can cut emissions by up to 90%. That's the supply chain equivalent of switching from deep frying to sous-vide—gentler on the environment, even if it requires more planning. Meanwhile, route optimization software and electric fleets are helping reduce Scope 1 and 2 impacts in last-mile delivery and factory operations.

Energy usage is another rich area for emission trimming. By transitioning to renewable energy sources—solar arrays on rooftops, wind credits, or direct power purchase agreements—many fabs are now baking sustainability right into their production lines. One chipmaker in Texas even installed a closed-loop cooling system that reduced water use and saved 1,200 tons of CO_2 annually. That's a lot of steam turned into clean air.

Finally, the future lies in **science-based targets**—carbon reduction goals aligned with the Paris Agreement's 1.5°C pathway. Like a Michelin-starred kitchen constantly chasing perfection, supply chains must set ambitious, auditable goals and report on progress with the same transparency as financials.

Carbon-conscious cooking is more than checking a box—it's a daily discipline. When sustainability becomes second nature, the result is a supply chain that performs better, costs less, and earns loyalty from eco-minded customers. Because, in the end, nothing tastes quite as good as a greener future.

Case Study - When Sustainability Became a Competitive Advantage

In the world of haute cuisine, presentation and provenance go hand in hand. Diners don't just want a delicious dish—they want to know where the duck was raised, who harvested the truffles, and whether that wine-paired fig was grown in a biodiverse orchard. The same shift is happening in global supply chains. Sustainability isn't just about doing the right thing—it's becoming a market differentiator, a badge of quality, and a source of long-term value.

Let's take a closer look at how **ASML**, the Dutch powerhouse in advanced lithography systems, turned eco-conscious innovation into a strategic weapon. While their machines are among the most complex in the semiconductor ecosystem—some valued at over $200 million—ASML recognized early on that its environmental impact extended far beyond its own walls.

Rather than focusing solely on internal operations, ASML launched a comprehensive **value-chain sustainability program**. This initiative required collaboration with hundreds of suppliers across the globe, with the goal of embedding energy efficiency, waste reduction, and material circularity into every tier. For instance, they began redesigning modules within their lithography systems to allow for **easy refurbishment and re-use**—cutting down on raw material consumption while speeding up turnaround times for customers.

To track and improve their efforts, ASML implemented **supplier sustainability scorecards**, measuring each partner's emissions reporting, energy use, water management, and labor practices. These scorecards didn't just incentivize better behavior; they became a gateway to deeper partnership. Suppliers who embraced eco-efficiency gained preferred status, early design involvement, and longer-term contracts.

The real breakthrough came when ASML connected sustainability to **performance and innovation**. One major supplier of high-precision lenses worked with ASML to shift to a closed-loop glass recycling system, dramatically reducing both waste and energy costs. In parallel, ASML invested in software to optimize machine energy consumption for customers—allowing chipmakers to reduce fab-level carbon footprints without compromising throughput.

The impact? Customers took notice. In an industry where precision and reliability reign supreme, ASML's commitment to sustainability became part of its value proposition. The company's environmental stewardship became a talking point during customer negotiations, a competitive edge in talent acquisition, and a cornerstone of investor relations.

ASML's story proves that sustainability isn't a garnish—it's part of the main dish. When embedded deeply, it drives collaboration, enhances brand equity, and unlocks operational efficiencies that ripple throughout the supply chain. It transforms the idea of "green" from a cost center into a center of innovation.

As this case shows, the most resilient, respected, and high-performing supply chains of tomorrow won't just be fast or lean—they'll be sustainable by design. That's a flavor worth cultivating.

Finishing Green: The Signature Touch of Sustainable Supply Chains

Sustainability may have started as a garnish—a well-meaning afterthought to the main course of profit and efficiency—but in today's supply chain kitchen, it has become a signature flavor. It's no longer just about reducing harm; it's about designing systems that nourish the business, the planet, and the people who make it all possible.

We've seen how responsible sourcing ensures every ingredient has a story worth telling, how waste reduction sharpens operations like a well-honed knife, and how emissions management adds precision and purpose to every logistical move. We've explored how bold companies like ASML have proven that green thinking isn't just good karma—it's good strategy.

But let's be honest—embracing sustainability isn't always easy. It demands more than checklists and certifications. It requires a mindset shift, a willingness to question the status quo, and the courage to invest in long-term flavor rather than short-term flash. Like fermenting a fine miso or slow-roasting the perfect broth, sustainability takes time, care, and consistency. But when it's done right, the results are undeniably richer.

The sustainable supply chain is no longer a niche trend—it's the new standard. It's where innovation and integrity meet, where transparency builds trust, and where doing what's right is also doing what's smart.

So here's to greener menus, cleaner kitchens, and supply chains that leave the world better than they found it. Because in the end, flavor fades—but values linger. And sustainability? That's a legacy worth leaving on the plate.

17

CRAFTING CULTURE - BUILDING A TEAM ENVIRONMENT

Stirring the Soul of the Kitchen - Why Culture Comes First

IN ANY HIGH-PERFORMING KITCHEN—OR semiconductor supply chain—there's something intangible that elevates the team beyond just doing a job. It's not just the SOPs, not just the schedules, not even the technology. It's the culture. The unspoken rhythm, the shared language, the mutual respect—the invisible seasoning that binds everything together.

Culture is the simmering stock that infuses every action with flavor. It's what makes someone jump in to help without being asked, own a mistake without fear, or push for improvement because excellence is the expectation—not the exception. In culinary terms, it's the difference between a chaotic kitchen and a Michelin-starred operation. In supply chain terms, it's what allows a cross-functional team to move as one—despite time zones, complexity, and curveballs.

In the semiconductor world, where speed meets precision and every move counts, culture shapes how decisions are made under pressure. It determines whether a delay becomes a blame game or a problem-solving party, whether employees feel like cogs in a machine or craftsmen at the bench, and whether leadership is feared, followed, or trusted.

Think of culture as the mise en place of your mindset. It must be prepped, organized, and cared for intentionally. You can't fake it with posters or slogans. You build it dish by dish, day by day, through consistent behavior, clear communication, and shared wins (and yes, shared failures, too).

One fab site in the Pacific Northwest once struggled with cross-department finger-pointing and high attrition. Leadership didn't throw more money or rules at the problem; they invested in listening sessions, rotating job shadows, and a simple "shift shout-out" board where teams could publicly recognize contributions from any function. In six months, productivity improved by 18%, and retention rates climbed. Why? Because people stopped feeling like parts in a process and started feeling like partners in a mission.

The best cultures aren't built on perks or ping-pong tables. They're built on purpose. They celebrate curiosity, reward initiative, and foster psychological safety. They empower the line cook to speak up, the planner to challenge the forecast, and the technician to propose a process tweak that ends up saving thousands.

So before we jump into frameworks or training programs, let's first acknowledge this: culture is the soul of your supply chain kitchen. If you get it right, your team doesn't just execute—they innovate. They don't just work together—they gel. And in the end, that's the real magic behind every five-star operation.

Hiring for the Kitchen - Recruiting with Purpose and Fit

Building a great team isn't just about finding people who can follow a recipe—it's about discovering those who can improve the recipe, add their own flavor, and keep the kitchen running when the heat's on. In both the culinary and supply chain worlds, recruiting with purpose is like choosing your brigade for the long haul. You want sous-chefs who challenge you, prep cooks who anticipate your next move, and stewards who protect the standards. It's not just about filling roles—it's about finding cultural ingredients that elevate the entire dish.

In semiconductor operations, the stakes are even higher. You're not just hiring for technical capability—you're hiring for trust, agility, and alignment with values that drive innovation under pressure. The wrong fit may look perfect on paper but can curdle the entire culture if they can't collaborate, adapt, or respect the team's rhythm.

Smart hiring starts with clarity. What kind of kitchen are you running? Fast-paced and experimental? Structured and disciplined? A hybrid cloud kitchen of global minds and time zones? Your environment should inform your hiring flavor profile. A lean fab team with minimal supervision needs self-starters. A cross-border NPI team may need cultural intelligence and collaboration superpowers over technical perfection.

One best practice borrowed from Michelin kitchens is the "stage" process—a working interview. In the semiconductor space, this looks like hands-on technical trials, cross-functional problem-solving exercises, or even collaborative whiteboarding sessions with future teammates. Not only does this test skill; it reveals temperament, curiosity, and coachability. Does the candidate listen like a prep chef during the dinner rush? Do they ask questions like someone who's hungry to learn the recipe, not just recite it?

Recruiting with purpose also means building diverse teams—because in a kitchen or a global supply chain, variety doesn't just add color; it brings resilience. Different perspectives catch blind spots, challenge groupthink, and spark innovation. Whether it's someone from a different industry, background, or part of the world, fresh eyes in the kitchen often see the bottlenecks others have normalized.

And fit? That's about more than personality. It's about mission alignment. Does this person want to be part of what you're building? Will they protect the standards when no one is looking? Will they keep service going when the oven breaks and half the staff calls out?

The truth is, every hire is a seasoning choice. Too bland, and your team lacks edge. Too overpowering, and you throw the dish off balance. But get it right, and you'll create a culture that simmers with potential—one role, one person, one perfect hire at a time.

Training the Team - From Knife Skills to Cross-Functional Chops

A well-trained kitchen doesn't just make great food—it hums like a finely tuned instrument, anticipating demand, correcting mistakes in real time, and working as one fluid unit during even the most chaotic dinner rush. The same applies to world-class supply chains. Training isn't a checkbox—it's an investment in adaptability, speed, and confidence. It's how a team turns from a group of specialists into a brigade that can flex across shifts, geographies, and crises without breaking a sweat.

In the world of semiconductors, the pressure to stay sharp is relentless. Processes evolve, technologies leapfrog, and supplier landscapes shift overnight. Training has to move beyond onboarding manuals and into the realm of continuous learning. Think of it like knife sharpening—if you're not actively maintaining the edge, you're letting it dull. And in this business, a dull edge can cut deep into efficiency, quality, and customer satisfaction.

Cross-functional training is the mise en place of modern manufacturing culture. When a planning analyst understands what's happening on the fab floor, or when a procurement lead can walk into an engineering review and speak the same language, the entire operation moves faster and with fewer misunderstandings. It's like a grill cook who also knows how to run sauté—when one line is overwhelmed, others can jump in and keep service flowing.

But training shouldn't be a one-size-fits-all buffet. The most effective programs are tailored, tiered, and hands-on. For operators, simulations and shadowing sessions turn theory into instinct. For managers, real-world case studies and scenario planning foster sharper decision-making. And for cross-border teams, cultural immersion and communication workshops build trust and fluidity across regions.

Modern tools are making it even easier to elevate skills on demand. Augmented reality (AR) systems can walk technicians through machine maintenance in real time, like a sous-chef whispering instructions during service. Digital twins and virtual simulations allow teams to practice decision-making in a no-risk environment. And AI-powered training platforms personalize learning paths based on individual performance, helping team members grow faster without overwhelming them.

But perhaps most important of all is creating a culture that encourages knowledge sharing. When team members feel empowered to teach others, celebrate learning, and admit gaps without fear, that's when the magic happens. It's no longer just training; it's transformation.

Training your team isn't about perfection. It's about preparing for pressure, instilling pride in the craft, and making sure that when the order board lights up with a hundred custom requests, your crew doesn't panic. They pivot. They plate. They deliver.

Because in the high-stakes world of global supply chains, the best teams aren't just trained—they're seasoned.

Recognition and Retention - Keeping Your Best Chefs on the Line

In any high-performing kitchen, keeping your top chefs isn't just about the paycheck—it's about respect, purpose, and pride. In the world of supply chains, the same holds true. Skilled talent is the secret sauce of any operation, and once you've found the right people, the challenge becomes keeping them inspired, appreciated, and committed for the long haul.

Retention isn't just about benefits and bonuses. It's about building an environment where employees feel seen, valued, and connected to the greater purpose of the organization. In semiconductor manufacturing, where even the smallest detail can affect multimillion-dollar outcomes, it's easy for individual contributions to get lost in the complexity. That's why strong recognition practices are critical—they keep the human element visible in a sea of data, wafers, and automated workflows.

Recognition can come in many forms: formal awards for perfect attendance or yield achievements, spot bonuses for innovative problem-solving, or simple public appreciation in a morning stand-up. The key is consistency and authenticity. Just like a head chef giving a nod of approval across the pass, the smallest gestures can feed motivation in powerful ways.

But there's more to retention than praise. It's about giving people a career path—not just a job. This means clear development plans, mentorship opportunities, rotational programs across departments, and learning platforms that empower employees to upskill on their terms. High-potential employees need to see that they're not just a cog—they're future leaders being prepped for the chef's table.

Companies that excel in retention also foster psychological safety. When people feel safe to speak up, share mistakes, or challenge a process without fear, they stay longer and contribute more. It's the cultural equivalent of a kitchen where even the dishwasher's feedback matters—because great ideas (and costly errors) can come from anywhere.

In the global supply chain arena, retention strategies must also adapt to different geographies and generational expectations. What motivates a millennial planner in Austin might differ from what retains a veteran technician in Penang. The secret is listening—really listening—and then tailoring recognition and career growth efforts accordingly.

And don't forget the power of storytelling. Highlighting employee contributions in company newsletters, intranet features, or all-hands meetings adds flavor to the organization's culture. It creates role models and inspires others to step up and shine.

At the end of the day, keeping your best chefs on the line means more than preventing turnover—it means preserving the flavor of your culture. When you celebrate talent, invest in growth, and serve up meaning with every task, your team doesn't just stay—they savor the work.

The Culture of Excellence - When the Kitchen Becomes a Family

Excellence isn't just a result—it's a culture. And in the most remarkable supply chains, it's not achieved through pressure or metrics alone, but through an environment where individuals feel like part of something bigger. Like a kitchen brigade that operates with silent choreography, a world-class team doesn't just function—they flourish. They move together, adapt together, and succeed together. That's what turns a workplace into a family.

At the heart of this transformation lies shared purpose. It's what turns a job into a calling and transforms KPIs into collective pride. In a semiconductor fab or a logistics hub, where the pace is relentless and the stakes are high, it's easy to become task-focused. But companies that cultivate a culture of excellence build rituals, language, and values that bind people—just like a restaurant kitchen that thrives not just on technique but on camaraderie.

This sense of family doesn't mean avoiding high standards. Quite the opposite. Kitchens with the strongest cultures are also the most demanding. But that demand is mutual. Teams expect greatness not just from leadership, but from each other. There's a deep-rooted accountability—not enforced from the top, but grown from within. It's the unspoken expectation that "we don't let the team down."

In global operations, where cross-functional and cross-cultural collaboration is the norm, fostering this unity takes intentional effort. Leaders become the chefs de cuisine of culture—setting the tone, modeling the behavior, and investing in traditions that bring people together. This could be as simple as team rituals (like "Win of the Week" shout-outs), recognition ceremonies, or shared meals that cut across departments and hierarchies.

Storytelling also plays a key role in reinforcing culture. When veterans pass down war stories of customer saves, production miracles, or wild recovery missions, they're not just reminiscing—they're handing down values. These tales become the folklore of the business, seasoning the air with pride and continuity.

The most magical cultures aren't accidental. They're curated with care. They hire for fit, nurture with feedback, celebrate progress, and never let excellence become stale. It's why some teams stick together for decades—across sites, product lines, or even companies. Because once you've cooked with a crew that has your back, everything else feels under-seasoned.

So here's to building more than a team—here's to building a kitchen where people feel like they belong, where greatness is the standard, and where every shift ends not just with results but with respect.

Because when your kitchen becomes a family, excellence isn't the exception; it's the house specialty.

Stirring Culture into Every Batch

A well-run kitchen doesn't just turn out dishes—it turns out discipline, camaraderie, and pride. Likewise, a high-performing supply chain doesn't just move parts—it moves people. Culture isn't a garnish; it's the roux at the base of every successful operation, the unspoken code that holds the team together when the pressure boils over, the orders back up, and the fryer goes down at the worst possible time.

From semiconductor cleanrooms to distribution floors, excellence isn't born from rigid manuals or generic mission statements. It rises from shared sweat, inside jokes, impromptu saves, and the knowledge that no one stirs the pot alone. That's what separates high-output organizations from high-impact ones—the invisible bond of trust, respect, and pride in the plate we all helped create.

The best teams? They know when to push, when to pause, and when to laugh through the chaos. They celebrate wins, own mistakes, and show up for each other again and again. Because in the end, it's not just about efficiency metrics or quality scores—it's about the people who make it all possible.

So build your brigade. Train with intention. Hire with heart. And lead like the chef who knows every name on the line.

Because when culture is done right, it doesn't just power the operation; it flavors everything.

And that, dear reader, is how the kitchen becomes more than a workplace; it becomes a home.

18

SCALING THE RECIPE - GROWTH STRATEGIES FOR EXPANDING SUPPLY CHAINS

Scaling the Recipe - Growth Strategies for Expanding Supply Chains

GROWING a supply chain is like scaling a beloved recipe from dinner for two to service for two hundred—complex, exhilarating, and fraught with new challenges. What worked beautifully in small batches can fall apart when multiplied unless the process is carefully measured, refined, and adapted. Growth isn't just about making more; it's about making more consistently, efficiently, and deliciously, without burning out your staff or your budget.

In the early days of any operation—whether it's a startup semiconductor fab or a boutique chocolate shop—the focus is often on survival: speed, hustle, and just-in-time creativity. But once you start expanding—adding new product lines, entering new markets, opening new facilities—that scrappy recipe needs to evolve. Your mise en place gets more elaborate. Your supply chain, once local and nimble, now stretches across geographies and time zones. And your tools need to evolve from hand mixers to industrial-grade robots.

Scaling successfully requires strategy. It means identifying which parts of your process are truly scalable and which need reengineering. You can't just throw more ingredients into a pot and hope for the best—volume changes everything. Temperature holds differently, timing shifts, and flavors can get muddled if you're not careful. Similarly, scaling a supply chain means re-evaluating lead times, supplier capacity, logistics routes, IT infrastructure, and talent bandwidth.

Take the example of a semiconductor assembly site that grew from regional to global distribution. Initially, components were sourced locally, with tight-knit supplier relationships and real-time communication. But as demand grew, so did complexity. They implemented tiered supplier networks, regional buffer hubs, and digital control towers to maintain visibility across continents. This allowed them to respond to demand surges, maintain quality standards, and still hit critical cycle times—without burning the dish.

It's also about understanding when and how to automate. Not every process needs a robot right away, but strategic automation—especially for repetitive or precision-critical tasks—can free up human capacity for innovation and problem-solving. Just like a kitchen uses automation for prep but keeps plating in the hands of chefs, your supply chain should be balanced between tech and touch.

And let's not forget leadership. As the team expands, communication becomes more complex. Cultural differences, remote teams, and varying capabilities demand not just structure but a shared vision. Think of it like expanding your kitchen staff—more hands help, but only if they follow the same recipe and trust the same head chef.

Scaling is both an art and a science. When done right, it elevates your operation from a brilliant single location to a globally recognized brand. When done wrong, it leads to waste, inconsistency, and disappointment on the customer's plate.

So sharpen your knives, update your prep lists, and make room on the pass—because growth doesn't mean changing the dish. It means perfecting it for every table.

Replicating Success - Playbooks, Processes, and Platforms

Scaling a great recipe is only half the battle. The real trick is replicating it—perfectly, consistently, and across multiple kitchens without losing the magic. Whether you're serving one region or ten, your supply chain's strength lies in its ability to repeat success. That's where the holy trinity of growth comes into play: **playbooks, processes, and platforms**.

Think of the playbook as your well-worn, sauce-stained cookbook—the one every sous-chef refers to in a crunch. It captures not just the "what" but the "how" and "why" behind your operational excellence. In a supply chain context, this includes standard operating procedures, quality benchmarks, escalation protocols, and proven vendor management tactics. A strong playbook eliminates guesswork when expanding to new geographies or integrating new products. It ensures that the spice level stays just right—no matter who's at the stove.

Processes are the mise en place of expansion. They bring structure and consistency, transforming creativity into repeatable excellence. Whether it's the steps for onboarding new suppliers, ramping up production lines, or transitioning to a dual-sourcing strategy, robust processes create a rhythm. They reduce chaos and empower teams to focus on agility and problem-solving—not firefighting.

One global electronics manufacturer, for example, scaled operations into Southeast Asia by creating a "site startup playbook" based on lessons from its Mexico and EMEA expansions. It covered everything from cleanroom setup and local compliance to sourcing packaging suppliers and qualifying automation vendors. The result? A 25% faster time to volume and smoother cultural integration—because the blueprint already existed.

Now, let's talk platforms—the digital backbone that holds everything together. Platforms are your smart kitchen appliances: cloud-based ERP systems, SCM platforms, digital twins, and AI-driven analytics. They enable visibility across borders, standardize data across sites, and ensure decision-making is guided by the same flavor of truth.

Platforms also facilitate **cross-site learning**. What worked in your Singapore fab can be instantly shared with your facility in Austin. Insights become recipes. Solutions become repeatable. Risks become manageable. Just like a restaurant franchise replicates ambiance, menu, and service across cities, your supply chain must replicate quality, responsiveness, and performance.

But be warned: replication doesn't mean cloning. Cultural nuances, local regulations, and resource availability mean you'll always need a dash of customization. The playbook provides the structure, but your chefs still need to taste and adjust for the local palate.

When playbooks, processes, and platforms align, they become your global prep team—ensuring consistency at scale, resilience in execution, and that unmistakable flavor your customers have come to expect.

People Scaling with Process – Growing the Team Without Diluting the Talent

Scaling a recipe isn't just about doubling ingredients—it's about ensuring the new chef knows how to season it just right. The same goes for expanding your supply chain team. As your operation grows, the challenge becomes clear: how do you bring in fresh hands without watering down the "secret sauce" of your culture, precision, and performance?

Enter **people scaling with process**—a strategy that ensures your growth story is powered by talent without compromising on quality. Just like in a bustling kitchen, every new hire must complement the existing crew, not clash with it. And they must be able to replicate the magic, not just follow the steps.

First, begin with clear role definitions and structured onboarding. Think of it like prepping your mise en place—each team member needs to know their station, their tools, and their responsibilities. In global supply chains, this includes understanding compliance standards, system protocols, escalation routes, and supplier nuances. Structured onboarding modules, paired with hands-on mentorship, help preserve institutional knowledge as new hires come in. It's like handing them the family recipe book with annotated tips from generations of chefs.

Second, standardize your performance expectations. Just as a line cook in Tokyo should plate the dish the same way as one in Texas, your procurement lead in Vietnam should manage vendors with the same rigor as their counterpart in Munich. Using digital playbooks, shared scorecards, and performance tracking systems ensures that core expectations are never lost in translation. Everyone follows the same rhythm, even if the ingredients differ.

Third, create career pathways and talent development pipelines. Growth without development leads to burnout and turnover—both costly ingredients to waste. Build in reskilling opportunities, leadership programs, and cross-functional rotations. It's like training a prep cook to run sauté and, eventually, the entire kitchen. That kind of agility becomes your competitive edge.

One semiconductor packaging company in Malaysia solved its scaling challenge by investing in a global "Supply Chain Academy." It blended online modules, job shadowing, supplier site visits, and simulations. The results? A faster ramp-up for new hires and a stronger bench of cross-trained talent ready to move between roles and geographies. Their fill rate for internal roles jumped 35%, reducing reliance on external recruitment and preserving their internal culture of excellence.

Lastly, don't underestimate cultural fit. Hiring for skill alone is like picking a chef based on knife speed but ignoring their taste. Align hiring with your core values—whether that's innovation, discipline, speed, or collaboration. Tools like behavioral interviews, peer reviews, and culture-fit assessments help ensure you're hiring team players, not just solo stars.

In the end, scaling people is about **amplifying your best qualities**, not just multiplying headcount. When done right, you don't just grow a team—you grow a brigade: unified, versatile, and ready to serve success on every plate, at every site.

Maintaining Quality at Scale - The Signature Dish at Every Location

Scaling is thrilling—new markets, expanded footprints, larger teams—but as any chef will tell you, **bigger kitchens don't always mean better food**. The real challenge is maintaining quality at scale—delivering that same signature dish with precision, whether it's plated in Palo Alto, Penang, or Prague.

In the culinary world, franchise chains know this all too well. A customer walking into a Paris location expects the same perfect croissant they had in New York. One slip in temperature, timing, or technique, and the brand loses trust. The same applies to supply chain operations. As you expand across geographies, suppliers, and production sites, **consistency becomes the gold standard**—and the hardest ingredient to replicate.

The first step is **standardization without suffocation**. Core operating procedures must be clearly documented and universally implemented, but with enough flexibility to accommodate local nuances. Think of it as a master recipe: ratios and processes are fixed, but spices might vary slightly to suit regional palates. In semiconductor supply chains, this often means global quality standards like ISO 9001 or IATF 16949 serve as the baseline, while regional teams adapt processes to match local supplier capabilities or labor laws.

Next, invest in **quality control systems that scale**. Digital quality management systems (QMS), AI-powered inspection tools, and real-time dashboards can offer centralized oversight across dozens of sites. If a facility in Korea detects an uptick in wafer yield loss, the central team in California should be alerted before the defect makes its way to customers. It's like having a sous-chef taste every dish before it hits the pass—quality isn't a checkpoint; it's a continuous pulse.

Cross-site **audit routines and peer reviews** also reinforce consistency. When teams audit one another—be it quarterly factory walks, line audits, or joint supplier evaluations—they exchange insights, identify deviations, and reinforce best practices. This mirrors how chefs rotate through stations to keep standards sharp and knowledge flowing.

Training plays a massive role, too. A foundry in Arizona once battled variation in die attach alignment between shifts. The issue wasn't tooling—it was technique. By implementing a global training module with video tutorials, VR simulations, and certification requirements, they eliminated variability and reduced rework by 40%. That's the power of investing in your cooks, not just in your kitchens.

And finally, **don't forget the taste test**. Even the best systems need a human touch. Regular feedback from customers, internal audits, and supplier scorecards ensure you're not just assuming consistency—you're proving it. Like any top kitchen, consistency builds reputation, and reputation builds revenue.

Scaling isn't just about multiplying outputs—it's about cloning excellence. When each plate, each part, and each process meets your gold standard, you don't just grow; you scale with soul.

The Role of Automation - Letting the Machines Handle the Repetition While You Focus on Flavor

Every seasoned chef knows that magic doesn't happen when you're peeling potatoes for six hours straight—it happens when your hands are free to innovate, experiment, and elevate the menu. In the world of supply chains, **automation plays the same role**: it liberates human creativity by taking over the repetitive, error-prone, and time-consuming tasks.

Think of automation as your **line cook that never sleeps**, never misplaces an ingredient, and executes every move with precision. In a small operation, handcrafting every component might be viable. But as your supply chain scales, manual processes become bottlenecks—slowing down output, introducing variability, and burning out your best talent. That's when it's time to hand the whisk to the robot and let your people focus on perfecting the recipe.

In semiconductor manufacturing, automation is not a novelty—it's an imperative. Automated Guided Vehicles (AGVs) now glide silently across fabs, ferrying wafers between stations with microsecond timing. Robotic arms execute die bonding and wafer dicing with a level of precision that the human hand simply can't match. And in distribution centers, AI-powered sorting systems handle thousands of SKUs with the kind of accuracy that would make a Michelin chef weep with envy.

But automation isn't just about robots on the floor. It includes **software automation** too: automated procurement processes that trigger POs based on inventory thresholds, scheduling algorithms that optimize machine uptime across multiple facilities, and predictive maintenance routines that flag tool degradation before it causes downtime. These digital sous-chefs keep your operations humming in the background—quietly but reliably.

A great example comes from a global chip assembly facility that was struggling with packaging line efficiency. Operators were performing repetitive visual inspections for packaging defects—a task that was both mentally draining and prone to inconsistency. After implementing a vision-based AI inspection system, they saw defect detection rates improve by 35%, and operator satisfaction jumped as workers were reassigned to higher-value roles like troubleshooting, programming, and process optimization.

The key to successful automation isn't just throwing robots at the problem—it's designing **human-machine collaboration**. Let the machines handle the chop-chop so your team can focus on the mise en place, on innovation, and on scaling up the dish without watering down the flavor. Just like a chef relies on timers, immersion circulators, or pasta rollers, supply chain leaders can use automation to achieve the same consistency, efficiency, and control—at scale.

At its best, automation becomes the invisible backbone of your operation—delivering reliability without removing the artistry. And that's how you keep flavor alive in a global kitchen, one perfectly timed process at a time.

Case Study - When Scaling Didn't Sacrifice Flavor

Imagine a small, artisanal kitchen known for one perfect dish—rich in flavor, balanced in texture, and revered by regulars. Now imagine that same dish being served flawlessly at a hundred bustling locations around the world. That's the challenge—and triumph—of scaling without compromising flavor.

Take the case of **ASML**, the Dutch powerhouse behind advanced lithography machines. Once operating with a boutique-level precision in a single site, ASML faced a daunting challenge: growing to meet exploding global demand without losing its signature quality or agility. The solution wasn't a frenzied rush—it was a deliberate recipe for scale.

ASML standardized its core processes into repeatable modules—think of it as templating the base of a signature sauce. They created detailed digital playbooks for suppliers, engineering, logistics, and installation teams. Instead of replicating entire facilities, they **scaled functions with surgical precision**—using automation and analytics to balance throughput without overwhelming capacity.

Their global supply chain expanded, but quality checkpoints didn't dissolve in the flood—they multiplied. Local teams were empowered to make decisions, but only after going through ASML's unique training kitchen. Every new facility became a clone, not in appearance, but in excellence, adapted to regional sourcing, compliance, and labor markets.

Meanwhile, they deployed AI to simulate future demand scenarios and identify bottlenecks before they occurred. Tools like machine learning algorithms and digital twins weren't just sprinkled in—they became key ingredients in sustaining scale. The result? ASML increased output by over 60% in five years, maintained customer satisfaction above 90%, and protected the precision of a machine that sells for tens of millions of dollars per unit.

But perhaps the biggest secret ingredient was cultural alignment. ASML didn't just scale machines—they scaled mindsets. Everyone from procurement to production line workers knew the importance of consistency, collaboration, and continuous refinement. It wasn't just about "making more"—it was about **delivering the same "gourmet experience" every single time.**

From One Kitchen to Many

Scaling isn't just a business move—it's a culinary transformation. It's the moment when a beloved neighborhood bistro becomes a global franchise without losing its soul. It's when a team takes what it does best, distills it, and replicates it with care, heart, and mastery.

In the supply chain world, growth without discipline is chaos waiting to boil over. But when you scale with intention—investing in people, preserving quality, and empowering through automation—you serve up something rare: a global operation that still feels artisanal.

So here's to the art of growth done right. May your processes be replicable, your teams inspired, and your "secret sauce" never diluted.

19

A DASH OF CREATIVITY: ENCOURAGING INNOVATION

Thinking Beyond the Recipe - Cultivating a Culture of Experimentation

EVERY ICONIC DISH began as a risk—a twist of ingredients, a break from tradition, a chef's intuition given room to roam. The same is true in the world of supply chains. While consistency keeps the kitchen running, it's creativity that elevates it to greatness. In today's high-stakes semiconductor and manufacturing landscape, innovation isn't just a garnish—it's the secret sauce for staying ahead.

But here's the truth: innovation doesn't happen by accident. It must be baked into the culture, not sprinkled on top like a garnish. A truly innovative supply chain is one where curiosity is welcomed, failure is forgiven, and new ideas are given the same reverence as a tried-and-true recipe. In other words, **we need kitchens that welcome experimentation**.

Think of companies like Intel and Nvidia—not just as tech titans, but as culinary innovators of silicon. Their breakthroughs in chip design, fabrication processes, and thermal management didn't come from sticking to old playbooks. They came from asking, "What if?" They empowered R&D chefs to try new flavors, even when the results weren't guaranteed. In one case, Nvidia's team prototyped dozens of GPU iterations before landing on a configuration that transformed graphics processing and unlocked an AI revolution.

To create a culture like this, you have to **design for discovery**. That means giving teams time to think, tinker, and test—whether it's through innovation sprints, hackathons, or dedicated labs. Just as a pastry chef needs downtime to perfect the next dessert, engineers and planners need white space to imagine better solutions. Organizations like Google and 3M famously carved out time for personal projects—leading to "Post-it Notes," "Gmail," and countless other hits.

Leaders must also model risk-taking. If your executive chefs never veer from the cookbook, why would the line cooks? Recognize the "good fails"—the prototypes that didn't work but taught you something new. And create safe spaces for cross-functional brainstorming, where procurement talks to engineering, operations shares with marketing, and suppliers are invited to co-create instead of just complying.

In the semiconductor world, where the pace of progress is rapid and unforgiving, innovation can't be left to chance. It must be systematic, structured, and celebrated. That means defining innovation KPIs, recognizing game-changing ideas, and showcasing successful "test kitchens" internally.

Because, in the end, the companies that thrive aren't just the ones with the best ingredients—they're the ones with the boldest chefs. They're the ones willing to taste, tweak, and reinvent.

So pull out the wild spices, sharpen those creative knives, and ask yourself, "What haven't we tried yet?"

Tools for Innovation - The Right Utensils for Creative Cooking

A great chef knows their tools. They don't just rely on a sharp knife or a sturdy whisk—they reach for immersion blenders, blowtorches, ring molds, and sous vide baths when the dish demands something extraordinary. The same applies to supply chain innovation. If creativity is the spark, then tools are what give that spark structure, speed, and direction.

In the ever-evolving world of global supply chains—especially in high-velocity sectors like semiconductors and advanced manufacturing—having the right innovation toolkit can mean the difference between staying ahead or falling flat. And we're not talking about the usual ERP or Excel spreadsheets. We're talking about the **molecular gastronomy gadgets of business**—the platforms, frameworks, and technologies that give your team room to play, test, and scale bold ideas.

Let's start with **digital sandbox environments**. These virtual testing grounds allow supply chain teams to trial new planning models, supplier strategies, or logistical configurations without affecting live operations. Think of it like recipe development: you're adjusting seasoning and texture before ever plating the dish for a customer. Digital twins—a simulated version of your end-to-end supply chain—make this even more powerful. Want to try rerouting a key supplier? Simulate it. Curious if additive manufacturing could eliminate a bottleneck? Model it first.

Then there are **collaboration platforms**. Tools like Miro, Slack, Microsoft Teams, and specialized innovation management software (like Brightidea or IdeaScale) allow ideas to move faster than an executive chef shouting "Behind!" across the kitchen. These platforms let teams sketch out concepts, vote on improvements, track progress, and invite input from cross-functional colleagues. When paired with agile methodologies and design thinking sprints, they become accelerators for real innovation—not just brainstorming.

Don't forget the power of **AI and machine learning** as creative sous-chefs. While these aren't "creative" in the human sense, they surface patterns and possibilities that humans may miss. From analyzing historical data to recommending alternative sourcing routes to predicting product demand under different launch strategies, AI serves up options that can fuel entirely new approaches. It's like having a tasting assistant who suggests ingredients you hadn't even considered.

On the supplier side, **open innovation portals** can transform the way you source ideas. Instead of treating vendors as mere executors, invite them to co-create. Ask them what they're seeing, what technologies they're piloting, and how you can experiment together. Some of the most game-changing supply innovations come not from inside the business but from partnerships beyond it.

Ultimately, building a culture of innovation isn't just about encouraging new thinking—it's about **enabling it**. The right tools empower every stakeholder to become part of the creative process. When that happens, your supply chain doesn't just respond to change —it invents what's next.

Empowering People - Letting Every Chef Create

In every great kitchen, there's an unspoken thrill when a line cook presents a clever twist on a classic dish or when a sous-chef improvises a plating technique that wows the room. Innovation doesn't always start from the top—it often bubbles up from the burners below. And in the world of supply chains, the same truth applies: real transformation happens when every member of the team feels empowered to stir the pot, add their spice, and experiment without fear.

Empowerment is the yeast that lifts innovation. Without it, creativity lies flat—undermined by rigid hierarchy, risk aversion, or a culture where the recipe is never to be questioned. But when you empower your team—across procurement, logistics, manufacturing, quality, and planning—you ignite a fire that fuels continuous improvement, adaptation, and bold thinking. Think of it as giving every chef the freedom to propose a new dish for the menu.

This begins with trust. Too often, supply chain teams are trained to execute, not to imagine. But when you give individuals ownership over their domain—encouraging them to challenge norms, suggest changes, and lead mini-pilots—you open the door to countless "aha" moments. At one fab packaging site in Malaysia, a technician on the floor developed a low-cost wafer clamping solution that reduced setup time by 15%. The innovation wasn't part of any strategic initiative—it emerged from someone who felt safe enough to speak up and curious enough to try.

Creating space for bottom-up innovation means more than putting a suggestion box in the cafeteria. It involves structured programs—like innovation labs, idea challenges, or cross-functional hackathons—that invite contributions from all corners. It means flattening decision-making layers so ideas don't get lost in bureaucracy. And it means celebrating not just the successful ideas but also the brave attempts that failed forward.

Recognition is key. Just like a kitchen celebrates the chef whose dish gets featured, your organization must spotlight internal innovators. Whether through internal awards, innovation showcases, or leadership shout-outs, the message must be clear: creativity is valued here.

Leaders play a critical role. By modeling curiosity, asking open-ended questions, and rewarding experimentation, they become the head chefs who cultivate a kitchen of innovators—not order-takers. One global materials supplier even instituted a "creative rotation" where employees spend a week shadowing different departments just to spark new perspectives. The result? Process breakthroughs, unexpected partnerships, and a surge in employee engagement.

Ultimately, empowering your people is about more than unlocking innovation—it's about creating a culture where everyone believes they have a hand in shaping the future. Because when every chef in your kitchen knows their ideas matter, you don't just cook; you create.

Creating a Culture of Experimentation - Where Mistakes Are Just New Recipes

In every great kitchen, there's a corner where creativity sizzles—where chefs try new spice blends, swap techniques, and plate up something unexpected. It's not always pretty, and it doesn't always work, but that corner is where culinary innovation is born. The same is true for supply chains. If you want to encourage innovation, you need more than tools and talent. You need a culture that treats mistakes not as failures but as "recipes in progress."

In semiconductor supply chains, where precision is prized and failure often equates to cost, embracing experimentation can feel risky. But risk is the price of discovery. Just as chefs test batch after batch before the perfect soufflé rises, supply chain teams must be encouraged to prototype, pilot, and occasionally burn a few ideas without fear of career-ending repercussions.

The most innovative supply chain organizations create what's often called a "test kitchen" environment. Whether that's a sandbox ERP to trial new workflows, a pop-up pilot line to test supplier materials, or a short-term logistics hackathon to explore alternative routing models, these are spaces where creativity gets cooked.

Crucially, these organizations build psychological safety. When a planner proposes a demand algorithm tweak, or when procurement trials a new sourcing method, leadership doesn't just permit it—they champion it. Innovation isn't handed down like a recipe card; it's developed like a new dish, through collaboration, iteration, and the occasional burnt pan.

Let's take Intel's Innovation Center in Malaysia as an example. There, cross-functional teams test advanced packaging methods and localized material substitution strategies in an agile, low-risk setting. These experimental efforts, many of which fail fast and early, have contributed to breakthroughs in speed to market and risk mitigation across Asia-based fabs. The secret? A culture where teams are applauded for trying, learning, and improving—not just for getting it right on the first try.

In the culinary world, chefs often say, "If you're not making mistakes, you're not trying hard enough." The same goes for supply chains. Innovation thrives in messy, iterative environments where feedback is fast and the cost of failure is low. It's about embracing the experimental mindset and baking it into daily operations—from new process mapping tools to supplier development programs.

Ultimately, creating a culture of experimentation means giving your team the freedom to play with the recipe. It means encouraging questions, testing assumptions, and celebrating the learning, not just the win. Because in the end, every five-star dish started out as a messy counter and a brave idea.

So go ahead—try something new. Let it flop. Then try again. That's where the magic simmers.

Case Study: Micron's Flavor Lab – Innovating at the Edge of Failure

Micron Technology, a global leader in memory and storage solutions, didn't earn its reputation by sticking to the standard recipe. In fact, its most game-changing innovations often started in what they affectionately call their "Flavor Lab"—dedicated spaces where cross-functional teams tinker, test, and trial the unimaginable.

One standout example is Micron's development of High Bandwidth Memory (HBM) packaging techniques. Traditionally, ramping up a new memory interface required lengthy validation, high investment, and rigid timelines. But by empowering small autonomous teams to experiment in parallel with core operations—much like a satellite test kitchen—they significantly accelerated their learning cycles. Failure wasn't a pitfall; it was a milestone on the path to improvement.

These "Flavor Lab" teams operated under a unique charter: break things fast, learn faster, and scale only what stuck. Engineers were encouraged to work with suppliers on rapid prototype materials, use 3D simulations to evaluate thermal performance in real time, and even test last-minute design swaps without wading through layers of approval bureaucracy. The result? A packaging advancement that shaved months off development timelines—and gave Micron a flavorful edge in a highly competitive DRAM market.

What made this possible wasn't just the tools or the tech. It was the cultural seasoning: leaders who rewarded curiosity, risk tolerance, and learning agility. They created space for failure—not as something to fear, but as something to measure and build upon. As one Micron engineer put it, "We weren't afraid to burn a few batches—we knew it was part of finding the perfect recipe."

This case underscores that innovation doesn't require a revolution—it requires an oven that's always on, a crew that isn't afraid to improvise, and a management mindset that says, "Let's taste and tweak."

Innovation Isn't Icing—It's the Batter

As we close the lid on Chapter 19, remember this: innovation isn't just a glossy garnish added at the end. It's baked into every layer of a world-class supply chain. It's found in the courage to test new ideas, in the tools that enable smart risk-taking, and in the cultures that applaud both triumphs and flops.

Just like a great dish evolves over time—through experimentation, feedback, and passion—so too does a great supply chain. And whether your team is developing the next breakthrough chip architecture or rethinking how goods flow across borders, the spark of creativity is what keeps your kitchen alive.

So, loosen the apron strings. Let your team stir freely. Taste often. Iterate without fear. Because the best recipes are the ones no one has dared to try—yet.

20

THE FINAL PLATE - FUTURE TRENDS IN SUPPLY CHAIN

The Chef's Crystal Ball - Peeking into Tomorrow's Kitchen

IN EVERY GREAT KITCHEN, there comes a moment when the service winds down, the last plate leaves the pass, and the chef begins thinking about the next menu. What flavors will trend next season? Which ingredients will become scarce? What new techniques might reshape how dishes are created and served? In supply chain strategy, we are now at that same reflective point—wiping down the counters, sharpening the knives, and peering into the simmering pot of the future.

The culinary chaos we've navigated—from supply shortages and global shutdowns to digital transformations and workforce reinvention—has brought us to a pivotal inflection point. The future of supply chain management isn't about restoring old rhythms; it's about composing an entirely new score—one that harmonizes speed, sustainability, personalization, and resilience.

One of the boldest shifts already underway is **hyper-automation**. While automation has long had a seat at the kitchen table, tomorrow's tech stack will extend far beyond robotic arms and automated forklifts. We're entering an era where "machine learning models" self-optimize, **digital twins train each other**, and **AI co-pilots** orchestrate real-time decision-making across procurement, logistics, and manufacturing. Think of it as replacing the sous-chef with an intelligent assistant who not only chops faster, but also reads Yelp reviews, forecasts demand, and suggests seasonal adjustments to the menu—all before you ask.

Then there's **supply chain as a service (SCaaS)**. Picture the cloud kitchen of the semiconductor world—a flexible, on-demand model where companies lease digital supply chain capabilities just like software. Smaller players gain access to big-league infrastructure, while larger organizations get scalability without investing in massive capital projects. It's Uber Eats meets "ERP data-rich" and is made to scale fast.

Meanwhile, **geopolitical shifts and climate volatility** are pushing the industry toward more **distributed, circular models**. Future-forward supply chains will be built like decentralized food trucks instead of central commissaries—closer to the customer, leaner on waste, and faster to pivot. Think micro-fabs, region-specific sourcing strategies, and dynamic inventory networks tuned for local flavors.

And of course, **sustainability** won't be a garnish—it'll be the base stock. From carbon accounting tools baked into ERP systems to full transparency on every link of the value chain, traceability and ethical sourcing will become the new table stakes. Companies will be measured not just on margin, but on impact. And those who plan now —who design green from the ground up—will earn the loyalty of a new generation of customers and investors hungry for authenticity.

The next plate isn't just coming—it's already being prepped. The question is: will you be the chef shaping it, or the diner waiting to be served?

The Rise of Predictive Everything from Forecasting to Self-Healing Networks

If yesterday's supply chain was about reaction, tomorrow's will be all about **anticipation**. Just like a seasoned chef who can sense when the béchamel is about to split or when the steak is five seconds from perfection, the future supply chain must act before the disruption hits, not after. Welcome to the age of **predictive everything**—where AI, data, and automation blend into an orchestration of preemptive action and continuous learning.

Gone are the days when forecasting meant poring over last year's sales figures and hoping for the best. In the semiconductor world, where lead times are long, demand signals are volatile, and market shifts can be triggered by a single tweet or trade policy, this kind of reactive approach is like tasting the soup after you've served it. Tomorrow's supply chains will be built on **real-time predictive insights** that constantly learn, adjust, and inform decisions before problems boil over.

Imagine a global wafer supplier receiving early warning alerts from integrated demand signals across OEM customers, social sentiment analytics, and even weather reports that forecast shipping lane delays. The system reroutes production, reshuffles logistics partners, and triggers alternate supplier readiness—all automatically. That's not science fiction; that's the direction in which the smartest kitchens are headed.

These **self-healing networks** function much like a sous-chef who notices the fryer is heating unevenly and immediately adjusts the oil, repositions the food, and alerts maintenance—all without pausing service. Sensors in cleanrooms, wearables on factory staff, and machine telemetry across fabs create a vast, integrated feedback loop. Predictive analytics flag anomalies before they become outages, while **digital twins** simulate the impact of rerouting production or reallocating labor with surgical precision.

In this world, **forecasting** becomes a living, breathing organism—constantly digesting inputs, sensing new patterns, and adapting recipes on the fly. Think of it as having a sommelier who knows your guests' preferences, the vintage availability, and even how the wine will pair with next season's menu—all before the first bottle is opened.

This predictive ecosystem is especially crucial for semiconductors, where demand surges can come from surprising sources—new smartphone launches, AI chip wars, electric vehicle mandates, or unexpected geopolitical bans. Companies that bake predictive capabilities deep into their planning systems will avoid the ingredient shortages and flavor misfires that derail unprepared rivals.

So, sharpen your data knives and train your AI palate. Because in this new frontier, success won't go to those who react best—it'll go to those who sense first and act**faster**, like a chef who already knows what the next dish should be before the customer even asks.

Future-Ready Skills - Training Tomorrow's Supply Chain Chefs Today

In the evolving kitchen of tomorrow's supply chain, success won't belong to the ones with the biggest ovens or the fanciest ERP—it will belong to those who've trained their chefs to cook in any kitchen, with any ingredient, under any condition. As automation, AI, and digital ecosystems continue to reshape the supply chain landscape, the demand for a **new breed of talent** is rising—people who can blend technical savvy with strategic thinking and a dash of creativity.

Think of it this way: you can hand someone the sharpest Japanese knife, the most high-end combi oven, and a pantry full of exotic ingredients—but if they don't know how to mix, measure, adjust, and innovate, the dish will fall flat. Similarly, tomorrow's supply chain professionals must be **multilingual in both data and operations**—able to read the metrics like a recipe card and improvise when ingredients run short or customer tastes suddenly change.

The shift is already happening. Traditional roles like "buyer," "planner," and "logistics coordinator" are evolving into **"supply chain analysts," "digital orchestrators," and "resiliency engineers."**

The most successful companies are already investing in upskilling and **cross-training** their teams. Programs in **data literacy, agile project management, scenario planning, and sustainability practices** are becoming as fundamental as Excel once was. Some leaders have even launched internal "supply chain universities" or "digital kitchens" to continuously reskill employees in emerging tech and adaptive leadership.

Just like every restaurant relies on its prep team before the guests arrive, organizations must prepare their workforce before the next disruption hits. Consider semiconductor manufacturers building talent pipelines not just in traditional hubs like Taiwan or Silicon Valley, but in Arizona, Vietnam, and Malaysia—ensuring regional agility and knowledge replication. Cross-border apprenticeship programs, remote collaboration skills, and AI-powered training platforms are becoming the new apron and spatula.

And let's not forget **culture**. A kitchen can only move as fast as its slowest cook, and a supply chain can only innovate as boldly as its most risk-averse team member. Building a culture where experimentation is rewarded, learning is continuous, and diversity of thought is prized will ensure the whole brigade grows together.

In the end, preparing tomorrow's supply chain chefs isn't just about headcount—it's about mindset. It's about cultivating **nimble, data-empowered, purpose-driven professionals** who are just as comfortable debugging an API as they are negotiating a supplier agreement or redesigning a forecast model.

Because in the high-stakes kitchen of global commerce, the future belongs to those who can adapt, anticipate, and always keep the flavor fresh.

Resilience by Design - Building for Disruption, Not Just Efficiency

In yesterday's kitchen, efficiency was king. Every movement was choreographed, every ingredient prepped just in time, every cost shaved like truffle over risotto. But the modern supply chain has learned the hard way—**you can't serve efficiency if the pantry is empty**. In today's high-stakes culinary arena, resilience isn't just a garnish; it's the main course.

Welcome to the era of **"resilience by design"**—a proactive approach where supply chains are architected not just to function in perfect conditions, but to flex, bend, reroute, and recover when the unexpected boils over.

It starts with **multi-sourcing**—the supply chain equivalent of knowing more than one way to make a sauce. Relying on a single supplier or region might offer the best cost per unit, but it's like betting your dinner service on one sous-chef showing up. When companies diversify supplier bases across geographies, they reduce the risk of natural disasters, political unrest, or regional lockdowns bringing production to a screeching halt.

Then there's **inventory strategy**. Lean may be in vogue, but lean without contingency is like cooking with a nearly empty fridge—any hiccup means improvising with condiments. Resilient supply chains design **dynamic safety stock models** that account for lead time volatility, customer priority tiers, and regional risk exposure. Think of it as building a walk-in pantry that adjusts itself with the seasons.

Digital twins—virtual replicas of supply chain networks—are also redefining risk readiness. These tools allow businesses to simulate disruptions in real time, test recovery scenarios, and optimize flows before any real-life crisis hits. It's like a chef testing ten new menus overnight in a virtual kitchen before committing a single carrot.

Resilience also means **investing in supplier relationships**. In high-trust partnerships, information flows faster, collaboration comes naturally, and problem-solving is collective. When the oven breaks, it's your vendor who rushes in with the spare part—because your success is baked into theirs.

And let's not forget the power of **localization and regionalization**. Global supply chains once prided themselves on complexity; now, many are rediscovering the value of proximity. Whether it's chip fabs in Arizona, final assembly lines in Malaysia, or micro-logistics hubs near consumer clusters—**decentralized networks offer agility and speed** that centralized giants often can't.

"Resilience by design doesn't mean abandoning efficiency—it means **redefining it**. Efficiency is no longer just about cost—it's about continuity. It's the ability to serve every plate hot, even when half the burners are out."

Because in the kitchen of global commerce, resilience isn't a backup plan—it's the recipe.

The Future Is Flavorful – A Final Forecast

Peering into the future of supply chain management is like eyeing a bubbling pot—you can sense what's coming, but the exact flavor? That's where the magic lies. What we do know is this: **the next decade will belong to those who treat change not as a challenge but as a cherished ingredient**.

Gone are the days of static playbooks and rigid frameworks. The future demands **fluidity, flavor, and foresight**. Companies will move beyond reacting to disruptions—they'll anticipate and adapt in real time, much like a seasoned chef adjusting heat and seasoning based on a quick taste mid-service.

We'll see **AI-driven orchestration become the norm**, with machine learning continuously tweaking forecasts, inventory levels, logistics routes, and production schedules. These digital sous-chefs won't just support decisions—they'll **co-create them**. They'll know the best supplier before you even finish your morning espresso and sense risk before the first tremor hits the trade routes.

Circular economy models will shift from nice-to-have to non-negotiable. Expect supply chains to extend their lifecycle lens, designing products for re-use, repair, and reinvention. Waste won't just be minimized—it'll be reimagined as a resource. From chip recycling to energy recapture in fabs, sustainability will be embedded in the recipe, not sprinkled on at the end.

Meanwhile, the **human element** will become more vital, not less. As automation handles the grunt work, the most prized skillsets will revolve around creativity, collaboration, critical thinking, and cross-functional fluency. We'll need supply chain chefs who can design across silos, lead with empathy, and make bold choices in ambiguous kitchens.

Geo-political flux, climate volatility, and demographic shifts will continue to shake the pantry shelves. But instead of clinging to brittle blueprints, tomorrow's supply chains will **lean into modularity, digital visibility, and data-fed intuition**—crafting strategies that bend, breathe, and bounce back stronger.

The final forecast? A vibrant, connected, resilient ecosystem—where agility is as fundamental as accuracy, where flavor matters as much as function, and where innovation is measured not only in margins but also in meaning.

So, as you hang up your apron on this final chapter, remember: the future isn't pre-written. It's cooked daily, crafted by teams who are curious, courageous, and unafraid to remix the recipe.

"May your supply chain be as flavorful as it is flexible—and always ready to serve what's next."

Final Reflection: Mastering the Menu

From your first mise en place to that final flambé, we've journeyed through a kitchen unlike any other—one lined with silicon instead of stainless steel, filled with sensors instead of spice jars, and staffed by data analysts, logistics coordinators, engineers, and procurement pros, all playing the roles of chefs, sous-chefs, and line cooks in the great restaurant of global commerce.

You've whisked through strategy. You've sautéed complexity. You've simmered through lean practices and pressure-tested your teams. Along the way, we've explored how creativity and control, much like salt and sugar, must be balanced to build a supply chain that doesn't just work—but wows.

Because the truth is, supply chain management isn't just about moving parts—it's about **mastering flavor at scale**. It's about knowing when to stick to the recipe and when to improvise; when to source the rare truffle and when to go farm-to-table with local partners; when to slow-roast and when to flash-sear.

In this culinary operations fusion, we've seen how a shared mindset can transform crisis into opportunity, how strong cross-functional teams can plate perfection under pressure, and how emerging technologies—when seasoned just right—can enhance rather than overpower your strategy.

But perhaps the biggest takeaway is this: **the kitchen never stops**. The orders keep coming. Customer tastes keep evolving. The ingredients change, the tools advance, and the expectations rise. And that's not something to fear—it's something to celebrate. Because in this chaos lies the chance to create, to lead, and to serve something truly unforgettable.

So whether you're overseeing a semiconductor fab in Taiwan, managing last-mile logistics in Texas, or reimagining procurement strategies from your global office in Singapore, remember this:

Every decision is an ingredient. Every team is a station. Every disruption is a chance to innovate. And every well-orchestrated supply chain is a meal worth savoring.

Thank you for taking this journey. Now get back in the kitchen—because the next course is always being written.

Agility. Flow. Simmering solutions. Served with style.

Bon appétit.

GLOSSARY OF CULINARY SUPPLY CHAIN TERMS

Amuse-Bouche: A small, flavorful introduction—used metaphorically for quick wins or pilot projects in supply chain.

Batch Cooking: Scaling operations for repeatability while maintaining quality.

Cleanroom Chef: Playful nickname for supply chain professionals orchestrating precision operations in semiconductor environments.

Commis of Compliance: The often-underappreciated heroes ensuring regulatory alignment across the sourcing table.

Flavor Transfer: Lessons learned in one area applied creatively to another.

House Style: A company's unique standard of execution—be it zero defects, on-time delivery, or ESG excellence.

Mise en Place: "Everything in its place"—the practice of organized preparation.

Plating: Final execution and presentation of a product or strategy.

Sous-Chef of Sourcing: The AI or analyst behind the scenes turning data into action.

Zero-Waste Kitchen: A mindset for circular design and sustainability in operations.

Resources

Industry Bodies & Certifications:

- ISO 14001: Environmental Management
- ISO 26000: Social Responsibility
- RBA (Responsible Business Alliance)
- IPC Standards for Electronics Manufacturing

Supplier Platforms & Tools:

- IMDS (International Material Data System)
- SCIP Database (Substances of Concern In articles, as such or in complex objects)
- EcoVadis ESG Ratings
- Resilinc Supply Chain Risk Mapping

Books & Reports:

- *The Everything Store* by Brad Stone (Amazon's supply chain evolution)
- *Supply Chain Management for Dummies* by Daniel Stanton
- McKinsey & Company: *State of Supply Chain Reports*
- Gartner: *Magic Quadrants for Supply Chain Tools*

Communities to Follow:

- Institute for Supply Management (ISM)
- Supply Chain Dive
- Women in Supply Chain (LinkedIn group)

Made in the USA
Coppell, TX
13 February 2026

71312542R00134